THE AMAZING GENIUS OF O. HENRY

CRITICAL AND BIOGRAPHICAL COMMENT

**Fredonia Books
Amsterdam, The Netherlands**

The Amazing Genius of O. Henry:
Critical and Biographical Comment

by
Arthur W. Page
Nicholas Fachel Lindsay
et al.

ISBN: 1-58963-554-X

Copyright © 2001 by Fredonia Books

Reprinted from the 1919 edition

Fredonia Books
Amsterdam, The Netherlands
http://www.fredoniabooks.com

All rights reserved, including the right to reproduce this book, or portions thereof, in any form.

In order to make original editions of historical works available to scholars at an economical price, this facsimile of the original edition of 1919 is reproduced from the best available copy and has been digitally enhanced to improve legibility, but the text remains unaltered to retain historical authenticity.

CONTENTS

	PAGE
LITTLE PICTURES OF O. HENRY	1
By Arthur W. Page	
THE KNIGHT IN DISGUISE	43
By Nicholas Vachel Lindsay	
THE AMAZING GENIUS OF O. HENRY	45
By Stephen Leacock	
O. HENRY: AN ENGLISH VIEW	70
By A. St. John Adcock	
THE MISADVENTURES IN MUSICAL COMEDY OF O. HENRY AND FRANKLIN P. ADAMS	79
O. HENRY IN HIS OWN BAGDAD	96
By George Jean Nathan	
O. HENRY—APOTHECARY	104
By Christopher Morley	
O. HENRY	105
By William Lyon Phelps	
ABOUT NEW YORK WITH O. HENRY	107
By Arthur B. Maurice	
O. HENRY AND NEW ORLEANS	137
By Caroline Francis Richardson	
"A YANKEE MAUPASSANT"—A SUMMARY OF THE EARLY CRITICISM	145
O. HENRY'S SHORT STORIES	151
By Henry James Forman	
THE O. HENRY INDEX	155

THE AMAZING GENIUS

LITTLE PICTURES OF O. HENRY
By Arthur W. Page

PART I—Born and Raised in No'th Ca'lina

IN Greensboro, North Carolina, at the time of Will Porter's youth there were four classes of people: decent white folks, mean white folks, decent "niggers," and mean "niggers." Will Porter and his people belonged to the first class. During the time that he was growing up there were about twenty-five hundred people in Greensboro. It was a simple, democratic little place with rather more intellectual ambitions than most places of its size, but without the hum of modern industry which the cotton mills have latterly brought to it or the great swarm of eager students that now flock to the State Normal School.

In this quiet and pleasant community William Sydney Porter grew up. Algernon Sidney Porter, his father, was a doctor of skill and distinction, who in late life practised his profession little, but worked upon many inventions. His mother is said to have written poetry and her father was at one time editor of the Greensboro *Patriot*. A President, a planter, a banker, a blacksmith, a short-story writer or a sailor might any of them have such forbears as these.

If any dependence can be laid upon early "influences" that affect an author's work, in O. Henry's case we must certainly consider Aunt "Lina" Porter. She attended to his bringing up at home and he attended her instruction at school. His mother died when Will Porter was very young, and his aunt, Miss Evelina Porter, ran the Porter household as well as the school next door, and a most remarkable school it was.

Porter's desk-mate in that school, Tom Tate, not long ago wrote the following account, for his niece to read:

"Miss Porter was a maiden lady and conducted a private school on West Market Street, in Greensboro, adjoining the Porter residence. Will was educated there, and this was his whole school education (with the exception of a term or two at graded school). There was a great deal more learned in this little one-story, one-roomed school house than the three R's. It was the custom of 'Miss Lina,' as every one called her, during the recess hour to read aloud to those of her scholars who cared to hear her, and there was always a little group around her chair listening. She selected good books, and a great many of her old scholars showed the impress of these little readings in after life. On Friday night there was a gathering of the scholars at her home, and those were good times, too. They ate roasted chestnuts, popped corn, or barbecued quail and rabbits before the big open wood fire in her room. There was always a book to read or a story to be told. Then there was a game of story-telling; one of the gathering would start the story and each one of the others was called on in turn to add his quota until the end. Miss Lina's and Will's were always interesting. In the summer time there were picnics and fishing expeditions; in the autumn chinquapin and hickory gatherings; and in the spring wild-flower hunts, all personally conducted by Miss Lina.

"During these days Will showed decided artistic talent, and it was predicted that he would follow in the footsteps of his kinsman, Tom Worth, the cartoonist, but the literary instinct was there, too, and the quaint dry humour and the keen insight into the peculiarities of human nature.

"The boys of the school were divided in two clubs, the Brickbats and the Union Jacks. The members of the Union Jacks were Percy Gray, Will Porter, Jim Doak, and Tom Tate, three of whom died before reaching middle age. Tom Tate is the sole survivor of this little party of four.

"This club had headquarters in an outbuilding on the grounds of the old Edgeworth Female College, which some years previously had been destroyed by fire. In this house they kept their arms and accoutrements, consisting of wooden battle-axes, shields, and old cavalry sabres, and on Friday nights it was their custom to sally forth armed and equipped in search of adventure, like knights of old from their castle, carefully avoiding the dark nooks where the moonlight did not fall. Will was the leading spirit in these daring pursuits, and many was the hair-raising adventure these ten-year-old heroes encountered, and the shields and battle-axes were oft-times thrown aside so as not to impede the free action of the nether limbs when safety lay only in flight. Ghosts were of common occurrence in those days, or rather nights, and arms were useless to cope with the supernatural; it took good sturdy legs.

"In the summer an occasional banquet was spread on the moss and grass under the spreading branches of the old oaks that surrounded the club house. On one such festal gathering ginger cakes and lemonade constituted the refreshments. The lemonade was made in a tub furnished by Percy Gray, and during the after-dinner talks one of the Sir Knights imprudently asked if the tub was a new one, and Percy replied in an injured tone: 'Why, of course it is; papa has only bathed in it three times.' To use an old quotation, 'Ah! then and there was hurrying to and fro and blanching of red lips and so forth.' . . .

"After the short school-days Porter found employment as prescription clerk in the drugstore of his uncle, Clarke Porter, and it was there that his genius as an artist and writer budded forth and gave the first promise of the work of after years. The old Porter drugstore was the social club of the town in those days. A game of chess went on in the back room always, and around the old stove behind the prescription counter the judge, the colonel, the doctor, and other local celebrities gathered and discussed affairs of state, the fate of nations, and other things, and incidentally helped themselves to liberal portions of Clarke's Vini Gallaci or smoked his cigars without money and without price. There were some rare characters who gathered around that old stove, some queer personalities, and Porter caught them and transferred them to paper by both pen and pencil in an illustrated comedy satire that was his first public literary and artistic effort.

"When this was read and shown around the stove the picture was so true to life and caught the peculiarities of the *dramatis personæ* so aptly it was some time before the young playwright was on speaking terms with some of his old friends. 'Alias Jimmy Valentine's' hit * is history now, but I doubt if at any time there was a more genuine tribute to Porter's ability than from the audience around the old stove, behind the prescription counter nearly thirty years ago.

"In those days Sunday was a day of rest, and Porter with a friend would spend the long afternoons out on some sunny hillside sheltered from the wind by the thick brown broom sedge, lying on their backs gazing up into the blue sky dreaming, planning, talking, or turning to their books, reading. He was an ardent lover of God's great out-of-doors, a dreamer, a thinker,

* This play is the dramatized version of A Retrieved Reformation. (See "Roads of Destiny.")

and a constant reader. He was such a man—true-hearted and steadfast to those he cared for, as gentle and sensitive as a woman, retiring to a fault, pure, clean, and honourable."

In these characteristics Will Porter followed in his father's footsteps. It was a saying in Greensboro that if there were cushioned seats in Heaven old Dr. Porter would have one, because of his charity and goodness to the poor. And there was an active sympathy between the old man and his son. The old gentleman on cold stormy nights when his boy was late getting home from the drugstore always had a roaring wood fire for him, and a pot of coffee and potatoes and eggs warming in the fire for his midnight supper.

This timid, quiet lad, who would slip around to the back door of "Miss Lina's," if there was company in the front of the house, held a little court of his own at the drugstore. He was the delight and pride of men two and three times his age. They still talk of the pictures he drew, the quiet pranks he played; but their greatest pride in him, as indicated above, is as a playwright. If you find one of that group now, and speak of O. Henry he will ask: "Did you ever hear of the play Will wrote when he was sixteen?" and then he will launch into laughing description of the little play written thirty-five years ago.

His pencil was busy most of the time, if not with writing, with drawing. He was a famous cartoonist. There are several versions of the story about him and an important customer at his uncle's store. Young Porter did not remember the customer's name, but when the man asked him to charge some articles he did not wish to admit his ignorance. So he put down the items and drew a picture of the customer. His uncle had no difficulty in recognizing the likeness. Perhaps one of the other versions of this story is the true one, but as they all unite upon the fact that he made a likeness that was accurate enough for his uncle to base his accounts upon, we may be certain that during his drugstore-club days young Porter was an adept at pencil mimicry as well as personal playwriting. It is as certain, too, that he dearly loved practical jokes. According to Mr. Charles Benbow, of Greensboro, "there was an old darkey by the name of Pink Lindsay who swept out the drugstore, made fires, and so forth. He was very fond of whiskey, and it took great care on the part of Will Porter and Ed Michaux, clerks, to keep Pink away from the whiskey used in prescriptions. They had a barrel of whiskey in the cellar and used a rubber tube to syphon the whiskey out of the barrel into a big bottle which was kept at the prescription counter. Notwithstanding the fact that the rubber tube was kept under lock and key old Pink or somebody was getting the whiskey. One day Will was in the cellar having Pink clean up the rubbish, and while sweeping down cobwebs he discovered two long straws hid on the wall of earth near the whiskey barrel. He said nothing. When Pink was out he examined the barrel and discovered a small hole bored into the top near the end of the cask. Immediately he divined how and where the whiskey went. He quietly took the straws upstairs and filled them with capsicum. He put them back exactly where he had found them. In those days we did not need pure food laws—capsicum was red pepper genuine. Pink was kept out of the cellar all day. The next morning being a cold one, Pink was both dry and cold. When Will sent him down cellar he was more than ready to comply. The cellar door opened out on the sidewalk and was one of those folding doors that when closed down act as a part of the sidewalk. It is usually closed as one goes down cellar. This time Pink happened to leave it open, and it was well for him. A few minutes elapsed and he let out a howl that would have done credit to a Comanche Indian. Yelling that he was poisoned, he made a bee line for the pump out in the street. Will pumped water for him until he could talk, and then he pumped the truth out of Pink about the straws. He was 'pizened,' and he was afire, and he promised never to use the straws again. All the while Will was as sober as a judge. He never smiled, and Pink did not suspect him."

In 1882 Dr. and Mrs. J. K. Hall went to Texas to visit their sons, Richard and Lee Hall, of Texas-ranger fame, and Will Porter was sent with them, because it was thought that the close confinement in the drugstore was undermining his health. He never again lived in

Greensboro, but Greensboro was never altogether out of his mind. Many years later, when he was living in New York, he wrote this account of himself—an account which gives an inkling of the whimsical charm of the man and his fondness for the old life in the old land of his birth.

"I take my pen in hand to say that I am from the South and have been a stranger in New York for four years. I am sometimes full of sunshine and at other times about as cross and disagreeable as you ever see 'em. But I know a restaurant where you can get real Corn Bread, clean, respectable, cozy, and draw the line at two things. I will not go to Coney Island and will not take walks on Sunday afternoons.

"It's a hard task to tell about one's self, for if you say too much you get turned down for an egotist, and if you don't say enough the man with the black moustache and side-bar buggy gets ahead of you.

"Now for something very personal and thrilling. It's about me."

(*The following paragraph was cut from a newspaper and pasted on the letter.*)

" 'He is a true soldier of fortune. He is still a very young man, but he has lived a varied life. He has been a cowboy, sheepherder, merchant, salesman, miner, and a great many other nameless things in the course of a number of very full years spent doing our West, Southwest, Mexico, South and Central America. He went about with a keen eye and supplemented it with a ready notebook, into which he jotted down his impressions and things that happened his way.'

"There are a few misstatements in the excerpt. I am not a 'very young man.' Wish I was. I have never been a cowboy, sheepherder, merchant, salesman, or miner. But I lived 'on the ground' with cowboys for two years. I never carried a notebook in my life. But here I plead guilty."

(*Here follows another newspaper clipping.*)

" 'He carried an abundant good fellowship and humour with him and saw the bright and amusing side of things.'

"Don't forget that I am the only original dispenser of sunshine.

"You may notice that I suppress my pen name in the quotations. I do that because I have been trying to keep my personality separate from my *nom de guerre* except from my intimate friends and publishers.

"I was born and raised in 'No'th Ca'lina' and at eighteen went to Texas and ran wild on the prairies. Wild yet, but not so wild. Can't get to loving New Yorkers. Live all alone in a great big two rooms on quiet old Irving Place three doors from Wash. Irving's old home. Kind of lonesome. Was thinking lately (since the April moon commenced to shine) how I'd like to be down South, where I could happen over to Miss Ethel's or Miss Sallie's and sit on the porch—not on a chair—on the edge of the porch, and lay my straw hat on the steps and lay my head back against the honeysuckle on the post—and just talk. And Miss Ethel would go in directly (they say presently up here) and bring out the guitar. She would complain that the E string was broken, but no one would believe her, and pretty soon all of us would be singing the 'Swanee River' and 'In the Evening by the Moonlight' and— oh, gol darn it, what's the use of wishing."

Part II—Texan Days

Will Porter found a new kind of life in Texas—a life that filled his mind with that rich variety of types and adventures which later was translated into his stories. Here he got—from observation, and not from experience, as has often been said, for he was never a cowboy—the originals of his Western characters and Western scenes. He looked on at the more picturesque life about him rather than shared in it; though through his warm sympathy and his vivid imagination he entered into its spirit as completely as any one who had fully lived its varied parts.

It was while he was living on the Hall ranch, to which he had gone in search of health, that he wrote— and at once destroyed—his first stories of Western life. And it was there, too, that he drew the now famous series of illustrations for a book that never was printed. The author of that book, "Uncle Joe" Dixon, was a prospector in the bonanza mining days in Colorado. Now he is a newspaper editor in Florida; and he has lately told, for the survivors of Will Porter's friends of that period, the story of the origin of these drawings. His narrative illustrates anew the remarkable impression that Will Porter's quaint and whimsical personality, even in his boyhood, made upon those who knew him.

Other friends, who knew him more intimately than "Uncle Joe" Dixon, saw other sides of Will Porter's character. With them his boyish love of fun and of good-natured and sometimes daredevil mischief came again to the surface, as well as those refinements of feeling and manner that were his heritage as one of the "decent white folks" of Greensboro. And with them, too, came out the ironical fate that pursued him most of his life—to be a dreamer and yet to be harnessed to tasks that brought his head from the clouds to the commonplaces of the store and the street. Perhaps it was this very bending of a sky-seeking imagination to the dusty comedy of every day that brought him later to see life as he pictured it in "The Four Million," with its mingling of Caliph Haroun-al-Raschid's romance with the adventures of shop girls and restaurant-keepers. At any rate, even the Texas of the drug-clerk days and of the bank-clerk period appealed to his sense of the humorous and romantic and grotesque. Here is what one intimate of those days recalls of his character and exploits:

"Will Porter, shortly after coming to Texas, became a member of the Hill City Quartette, of Austin, composed of C. E. Hillyer, R. H. Edmundson, Howard Long, and himself. Porter was the littlest man in the crowd, and, of course, basso profundo. He was about five feet six inches tall, weighed about one hundred and thirty pounds, had coal black hair, gray eyes, and a long, carefully twisted moustache; looked as though he might be a combination between the French and the Spanish, and I think he once told me that the blood of the Huguenot flowed in his veins. He was one of the most accomplished gentlemen I ever knew. His voice was soft and musical, with just enough rattle in it to rid it of all touch of effeminacy. He had a keen sense of humour, and there were two distinct methods of address which were characteristic with him—his business address and his friendly address. As a business man, his face was calm, almost expressionless; his demeanour was steady, even calculated. He always worked for a high class of employers, was never wanting for a position, and was prompt, accurate, talented, and very efficient; but the minute he was out of business—that was all gone. He always approached a friend with a merry twinkle in his eye and an expression which said: 'Come on, boys, we are going to have a lot of fun,' and we usually did.

"The story of The Green Door * in its spirit and in its fact was just such a thing as might happen with him any night. It is but justice, in order to give balance to this unique character, to say that he made no reli-

* See "The Four Million."

gious professions; he never talked infidelity nor scepticism; he had such a reverence for other people's views that he never entered into religious discussions; and personally he seemed rather indifferent to the subject, though in no wise opposed to it. He rarely ever missed church, and the Hill City Quartette were nearly always to be found in either the Baptist or the St. David's Episcopal Church choirs, though he usually attended church on Sunday evenings at the Presbyterian Church and sang in their choir.

"He got interested in society and lost all taste for the drug business. Being a fine penman, a good accountant, well educated, and with good address, it was an easy matter for him to make a living without working every day and Sunday, too, and most of the evenings besides. The fact of the matter is, while W. S. P. would not have admitted it for the world, I think he really wanted a little more time for love-making. So during the time of our association, he went to work at eight in the morning and quit at four. He always had sufficient money for what he needed; if he had any more, no one knew it. He was very fond of going fishing, but he let you do the fishing after he went. He loved to go hunting, but he let you kill the birds, and somehow I always thought that on these trips he got something out of the occasion that he enjoyed all by himself; they were not occasions which invited the introduction of sentiment, yet I believe his enjoyment of them was purely sentimental. He loved the mountains and the plains; he loved to hear the birds sing and the brooks babble, and all those things, but he did not talk to the boys about it.

"He was accomplished in all the arts of a society man; had a good bass voice and sang well; was a good dancer and skater; played an interesting game of cards, and was preëminently an entertainer. There were no wall flowers to Porter, and the girl who went with him never lacked for attention.

"The Hill City Quartette formed the centre of the Social Circle in which W. S. P. was the central figure during the period of this writing.

"If W. S. P. at this time had any ambitions as a writer, he never mentioned it to me. I do not recall that he was fond of reading. One day I quoted some lines to him from a poem by John Alexander Smith. He made inquiry about the author, borrowed the book, and committed to memory a great many passages from it, but I do not recall ever having known him to read any other book. I asked him one day why he never read fiction. His reply was: 'That it was all tame compared with the romance in his own life,'—which was really true.

"Mr. Porter was very careful in the use and selection of language. He rarely used slang, and his style in ordinary conversation was very much purer and more perfect than it is in his writings. This can be accounted for in the fact that he was an unusually polished gentleman, but writing in the first person, the character which he selects to represent himself appears to be along a much lower and commoner line than he himself actually lived; but, on the other hand, the stories that he writes and the quaint way he has of putting things were largely characteristic of his personal daily life, and the peculiar turn that he gives to his stories—in which he leads you to think along logical lines until you think you have anticipated his conclusion, then suddenly brings the story to a reasonable but wholly unexpected conclusion—was even in this early day an element in his common conversation.

"In the great railroad strike at Fort Worth, Texas, the Governor called out the State Militia, and the company to which we belonged was sent, but as we were permitted a choice in the matter, Porter and I chose not to go. In a little while a girl he was in love with went to Waco on a visit. Porter moped around disconsolate for a few days, and suddenly said to me: 'I believe I'll take a visit at the Government's expense.' With him to think was to act. A telegram was sent to Fort Worth: 'Capt. Blank, Fort Worth, Texas. Squad of volunteers Company Blank, under my command, tender you their services if needed. Reply.' 'Come next train,' Captain Blank commanded. Upon reaching the depot no orders for transportation of squad had been received. Porter actually held up the train until he could telegraph and get transportation for his little squad, because the girl had been notified that he would be in Waco on a certain train. She afterward said that when the train pulled into Waco he was sitting on the engine pilot with a gun across his lap and a distant glance at her was all that he got, but he had had his adventure and was fully repaid.

"This adventure is only one of thousands of such incidents that commonly occurred in his life. He lived in an atmosphere of adventure that was the product of his own imagination. He was an inveterate storyteller, seemingly purely from the pleasure of it, but he never told a vulgar joke, and as much as he loved humour he would not sacrifice decency for its sake, and his stories about women were always refined.

"He told a great many stories in the first person. We were often puzzled to know whether they were real or imaginary, and when we made inquiry his stock reply was: 'Never question the validity of a joke.'

"One night at the Lampasas Military Encampment of Texas Volunteer Guards, the Quartette, with others, had leave of absence to attend the big ball at the Park Hotel, with orders to report at 12:00 sharp. Somehow, with girls and gaiety and music and balmy Southern breezes and cooing voices, time flies, and before any of us had thought to look at a watch it was five minutes past twelve and we were in trouble. We had all gathered near the doorway looking toward Camp when we saw the Corporal of the Guard approaching the building to arrest us. Of course, what follows could never have happened in a camp of tried veterans, but Porter knew the human animal as few people do.

He got a friend with an unlimited leave of absence to meet the Corporal's squad at another door and suggest to them that they should not carry the guns in among the ladies. So the squad stacked their guns on the outside and went into the other door to arrest us. Up to this point Porter had worked the thing without taking us into his confidence. As soon as the guns were stacked he beckoned us to follow and we did not stop for explanation. We knew where Porter led there would be adventure, if not success. He took command; we unstacked the arms of the corporal's squad; all our boys who did not carry guns were marched as under arrest. Now none of us knew the countersign, and our success in getting by the sentry was a matter of pure grit. As we approached the sentry we were crossing a narrow plank bridge in single file, at the end of which the sentry threw up his gun and Porter marched us right straight up to that gun until the front man was marking time with the point of the gun right against his stomach. Porter just said to the sentry, 'Squad under arrest. Stand aside!' The whole thing was done with such courage, decision, and audacity, that the sentry never noticed that we had not given the countersign, but stepped aside and let us pass. A few yards into the camp we stacked our guns, and sneaked into our tents. When the real corporal and squad came back to camp and told his story the sentry refused to accept it and had the whole squad placed in the guardhouse for the night. When the boys began to whisper the joke to their comrades in their tents, the disturbance became so great that the Corporal's Guard came down to ascertain the cause of the disturbance, but on looking into the tent found only tired soldier boys snoring as though they had been drugged. There was quite a time at the court-martial next morning, at which the Corporal and his body were given extra duty for their inglorious behaviour on the previous night, but no one ever knew our connection with the story."

But the lure of the pen was getting too strong for Will Porter to resist. Life as a teller in the First National Bank of Austin was too routine not to be relieved by some outlet for his love of fun and for his creative literary instinct. An opportunity opened to buy a printing outfit, and he seized it and used it for a year to issue the *Rolling Stone*, a weekly paper that suggested even then his later method as a humourist and as a photographic portrayer of odd types of humanity. Dr. D. Daniels—"Dixie" he was to Will Porter—now a dentist in Galveston, Texas, was his partner in this enterprise, and his story of that year of fun gives also a picture of Will Porter's habit of studying human nature at first hand—a habit that later carried him into many quaint byways of New York and into many even more quaint and revealing byways of the human heart. Here is Dr. Daniels's story:

"It was in the spring of 1894 that I floated into

Austin," said Daniels, "and I got a place in the State printing office. I had been working there for a short time when I heard that a man named Porter had bought out the old *Iconoclast* plant—known everywhere as Brann's *Iconoclast*—and was looking for a printer to go into the game with him. I went around to see him, and that was the first time I met O. Henry. Porter had been a clerk in the Texas Land Office and a teller in the First National Bank in Austin, and when W. C. Brann went to Waco decided to buy out his plant and run a weekly humorous paper.

"I talked things over with him, the proposition looked good, and we formed a partnership then and there. We christened the paper the *Rolling Stone* after a few discussions, and in smaller type across the full-page head we printed 'Out for the moss.' Which is exactly what we were out for. Our idea was to run this weekly with a lot of current events treated in humorous fashion, and also to run short sketches, drawings, and verse. I had been doing a lot of chalk-plate work and the specimens I showed seemed to make a hit with Porter. Those chalk-plates were the way practically all of our cuts were printed.

"Porter was one of the most versatile men I had ever met. He was a fine singer, could write remarkably clever stuff under all circumstances, and was a good hand at sketching. And he was the best mimic I ever saw in my life. He was one of the genuine democrats that you hear about more often than you meet. Night after night, after we would shut up shop, he would call to me to come along and 'go bumming.' That was his favourite expression for the night-time prowling in which we indulged. We would wander through streets and alleys, meeting with some of the worst specimens of down-and-outers it has ever been my privilege to see at close range. I've seen the most ragged specimen of a bum hold up Porter, who would always do anything he could for the man. His one great failing was his inability to say 'No' to a man.

"He never cared for the so-called 'higher classes' but watched the people on the streets and in the shops and cafés, getting his ideas from them night after night. I think that it was in this way he was able to picture the average man with such marvellous fidelity.

"Well, as I started to say, we moved into the old *Iconoclast* plant, got out a few issues, and moved into the Brueggerhoff Building. The *Rolling Stone* met with unusual success at the start, and we had in our files letters from men like Bill Nye and John Kendrick Bangs praising us for the quality of the sheet. We were doing nicely, getting the paper out every Saturday—approximately—and blowing the gross receipts every night. Then we began to strike snags. One of our features was a series of cuts with humorous underlines of verse. One of the cuts was the rear view of a fat German professor leading an orchestra, beating the air wildly with his baton. Underneath the cut Porter had written the following verse:

With his baton the professor beats the bars,
  'Tis also said he beats them when he treats.
But it made that German gentleman see stars
  When the bouncer got the cue to bar the beats.

"For some reason or other that issue alienated every German in Austin from the *Rolling Stone*, and cost us more than we were able to figure out in subscriptions and advertisements.

"Another mistake Porter made was when he let himself be dragged into a San Antonio political fight—the O'Brien-Callaghan mayoralty campaign. He was pulled into this largely through a broken-down English writer, whose name, as I remember, was Henry Rider Taylor. How Taylor had any influence over him I never was able to make out, for he used constantly to make fun of him. 'Here comes that man Taylor,' he'd say. 'Got a diamond on him as big as a two-bit piece and shinin' like granulated sugar.' But he went into the political scrap just the same, and it cost him more than it was worth.

"We got out one feature of the paper that used to meet with pretty general approval. It was a page gotten up in imitation of a backwoods country paper, and we christened it *The Plunkville Patriot*. That idea has been carried out since then in a dozen different forms, like *The Hogwallow Kentuckian*, and *The Bingville Bugle*, to give two of the prominent examples. Porter and I used to work on this part of the paper nights and Sundays. I would set the type for it, as there was a system to all of the typographical errors that we made, and I couldn't trust any one else to set it up as we wanted it.

"Porter used to think up some right amusing features for this part of the paper. I remember that about then we had on hand a lot of cuts of Gilmore, of Gilmore's Band, which played at the dedication of the State capitol at Austin. We would run these cuts of Gilmore for any one, from Li Hung Chang to Governor Hogg.

"The Populist Party was coming in for all sorts of publicity at this time, and the famous 'Sockless' Simpson, of Kansas, was running for Congress. Porter worked out a series of 'Tictocq, the Great French Detective,' in burlesque of 'Lecoq,' and in one story, I remember, had a deep-laid conspiracy to locate a pair of socks in Simpson's luggage, thus discrediting him with his political following.

"The paper ran along for something over a year, and then was discontinued. Following the political trouble and the other troubles in which Porter became involved, he left the State. Some time was spent in Houston; the next stop was New Orleans; then he jumped to South America, and only returned to Texas for a short period before leaving the State forever. His experiences on a West Texas ranch, in Texas cities and in South America, however, gave him a thorough insight into the average run of people whom he pictured so vividly in his later work. He was a greater man than any of us knew when we were with him in the old days."

III—The New York Days—*Richard Duffy's narrative*

His coming to New York, with the resolution "to write for bread," as he said once in a mood of acrid humour, was dramatic, as is a whisper compared to a subdued tumult of voices. I believe I am correct in saying that outside his immediate family few were aware that O. Henry was entering this "nine-day town" except Gilman Hall, my associate on *Ainslee's Magazine*, the publishers, Messrs. Street and Smith, and myself. For some time we had been buying stories from him, written in his perfect Spencerian copperplate hand that was to become familiar to so many editors. Only then he wrote always with a pen on white paper, whereas once he was established in New York he used a lead pencil sharpened to a needle's point on one of the yellow pads that were always to be seen on his table. The stories he published at this period were laid either in the Southwest or in Central America, and those of the latter countries form the bulk of his first issued volume, "Cabbages and Kings." It was because we were sure of him as a writer that our publishers willingly advanced the cheque that brought him to New York and assured him a short breathing spell to look round and settle. Also, it was because O. Henry wanted to come. You could always make him do anything he wanted to do, as he had a way of saying, if you were coaxing him into an invitation he had no intention of pursuing into effect.

It was getting late on a fine spring afternoon down at Duane and William streets when he came to meet us. From the outer gate the boy presented a card bearing the name William Sydney Porter. I don't remember just when we found out that "O. Henry" was merely a pen name; but think it was during the correspondence arranging that he come to New York. I do remember, however, that when we were preparing our yearly prospectus, we had written to him, asking that he tell us what the initial O. stood for, as we wished to use his photograph and preferred to have his name in full. It was the custom and would make his name stick faster in the minds of readers. With a courteous flourish of appreciation at the honour we were offering him in making him known to the world, he sent us "Olivier," and so he appeared as Olivier Henry in the first publishers' announcement in which his stories were heralded. Later he confided to us, smiling, what a lot of fun he had had in picking out a first name of sufficient advertising effectiveness that began with O.

As happens in these matters, whatever mind picture Gilman Hall or I had formed of him from his letters, his handwriting, his stories, vanished before the impression of the actual man. He wore a dark suit of clothes, I recall, and a four-in-hand tie of bright colour. He carried a black derby, high-crowned, and walked with a springy, noiseless step. To meet him for the first time you felt his most notable quality to be reticence, not a reticence of social timidity, but a reticence of deliberateness. If you also were observing, you would soon understand that his reticence proceeded from the fact that civilly yet masterfully he was taking in every item of the "you" being presented to him to the accompaniment of convention's phrases and ideas, together with the "you" behind this presentation. It was because he was able thus to assemble and sift all the multifarious elements of a personality with sleight-of-hand swiftness that you find him characterizing a person or a neighbourhood in a sentence or two; and once I heard him characterize a list of editors he knew each in a phrase.

On his first afternoon in New York we took him on our usual walk uptown from Duane Street to about Madison Square. That was a long walk for O. Henry, as any who knew him may witness. Another long one was when he walked about a mile over a fairly high hill with me on a zigzag path through autumn woods. I showed him plains below us and hills stretching away so far and blue they looked like the illimitable sea from the deck of an ocean liner. But it was not until we approached the station from which we were to take the train back to New York that he showed the least sign of animation. "What's the matter, Bill?" I asked, "I thought you'd like to see some real country." His answer was: "Kunn'l, how kin you expeck me to appreciate the glories of nature when you walk me over a mounting like that an' I got new shoes on?" Then he stood on one foot and on the other, caressing each aching member for a second or two, and smiled with bashful knowingness so like him.

It was one of his whimsical amusements, I must say here, to speak in a kind of country style of English, as though the English language were an instrument he handled with hesitant unfamiliarity. Thus it happened that a woman who had written to him about his stories and asked if her "lady friend" and she might meet him, informed him afterward: "You mortified me nearly to death, you talked so ungrammatical!"

We never knew just where he stopped the first night in New York, beyond his statement that it was at a hotel not far from the ferry in a neighbourhood of so much noise that he had not been able to sleep. I suppose we were voluminous with suggestions as to where he might care to live, because we felt we had some knowledge of the subject of board and lodging, and because he was the kind of man you'd give your best hat to on short acquaintance, if he needed a hat—but also he was the kind of man who would get a hat for himself. Within about twenty-four hours he called at the office again to say that he had taken a large room in a French table d'hôte hotel in Twenty-fourth Street, between Broadway and Sixth Avenue. Moreover, he brought us a story. In those days he was very prolific. He wrote not only stories, but occasional skits and light verse. In a single number of *Ainslee's*, as I remember, we had three short stories of his, one of which was signed "O. Henry" and the other two with pseudonyms. Of the latter, While the Auto Waits,* was picked out by several newspapers outside New York as an unusually clever short story. But as O. Henry naturally he appeared most frequently, as frequently as monthly publication allows, for to my best recollection of the many stories we saw of his there were only three about which we said to him we would rather have another instead.

Still he lived in West Twenty-fourth Street, although the place had no particular fascination for him. We used to see him every other day or so, at luncheon, at dinner, or in the evening. Various magazine editors began to look up O. Henry, which was a job somewhat akin to tracing a lost person. While his work was coming under general notice rapidly, he made no effort to push himself into general acquaintance; and all who knew him when he was actually somewhat of a celebrity should be able to say that it was about as easy to induce him to "go anywhere" to meet somebody as it is to have a child take medicine. He was persuaded once to be the guest of a member of the Periodical Publishers' Association on a sail up the Hudson; but when the boat made a stop at Poughkeepsie, O. Henry slipped ashore and took the first train back to New York. Yet he was not unsociable, but a man that liked a few friends round him and who dreaded and avoided a so-called "party" as he did a crowd in the subway.

It was at his Twenty-fourth Street room that Robert

* See "Voice of the City."

H. Davis, then of the staff of the New York *World*, ran him to cover, as it were, and concluded a contract with him to furnish one story a week for a year at a fixed salary. It was a gigantic task to face, and I have heard of no other writer who put the same quality of effort and material in his work able to produce one story every seven days for fifty-two successive weeks. The contract was renewed, I believe, and all during this time O. Henry was selling stories to magazines as well. His total of stories amounts to two hundred and fifty-one, and when it is considered that they were written in about eight years, one may give him a good mark for industry, especially as he made no professional vaunt about "loving his work." Once, when dispirited, he said that almost any other way of earning a living was less of a toil than writing. The mood is common to writers, but not so common as to happen to a man who practically had editors or agents of editors sitting on his doorstep requesting copy.

When he undertook his contract with the *World* he moved to have more room and more comfortable surroundings for the new job. But he did not move far, no farther than across Madison Square, in East Twenty-fourth Street, to a house near Fourth Avenue. Across the street stands the Metropolitan Building, although it was not so vast then. He had a bedroom and sitting-room at the rear of the parlour floor with a window that looked out on a typical New York yard, boasting one ailanthus tree frowned upon by time-stained extension walls of other houses. More and more men began to seek him out, and he was glad to see them, for a good deal of loneliness enters into the life of a man that writes fiction during the better part of the day, and when his work is over feels he must move about somewhere to gather new material. Here it was that he received a visit one day from a stranger, who announced that he was a business man, but had decided to change his line. He meant to write stories, and having read several of O. Henry's, he was convinced that kind of story would be the best paying proposition. O. Henry liked the man off-hand, but he could not help being amused at his attitude toward a "literary career." I asked what advice he gave the visitor, and he answered: "I told him to go ahead!" The sequel no doubt O. Henry thoroughly enjoyed, for within a few years the stranger had become a best-seller, and continues such.

O. Henry remained only for a few months in these lodgings, having among a dozen reasons for moving the fact that he had more money.

I follow his movings with his trunks, his bags, his books, a few, but books he read, and his pictures, likewise a few, that were original drawings presented to him, or some familiar printed picture that had caught his fancy, because in his movings you trace his life in New York. His next abiding-place was at 55 Irving Place, as he has said in a letter, "a few doors from old

Wash. Irving's house." Here he had almost the entire parlour floor with a window large as a store front, opening only at the sides in long panels. At either one of these panels he would sit for hours watching the world go by along the street, not gazing idly, but noting men and women with penetrating eyes, making guesses at what they did for a living, and what fun they got out of it when they had earned it.

He was a man you could sit with a long while and feel no necessity for talking; but every so often a passerby would evoke a remark from him that converted an iota of humanity into the embryo of a story. Although he spoke hardly ever to any one in the house except the people who managed it, he had the lodgers all ticketed in his mind. He was friendly but distant with persons of the neighbourhood he was bound to meet regularly, because he lived so long there, and I have often thought he must have persisted as a mysterious man to them simply because he was so far from being communicative.

From Irving Place he went back across the Square to live in a house next to the rectory of Trinity Chapel in West Twenty-fifth Street. But now he moved because the landlady and several lodgers were moving to the same house. From here his next change was to the Caledonia, in West Twenty-sixth Street, whence, as everybody knows he made his last move to the Polyclinic Hospital, where he died.

PART IV—As He Showed Himself in His Letters

Collections of material about an author are not respecters of chronology, and in the material concerning O. Henry, assembled chiefly by the energy of the late Harry Peyton Steger, are many curious contrasts—little printed rejection slips from Sunday newspapers of an early date keeping company with long and appreciative letters of later date from magazine editors, and clippings from the London *Spectator* comparing O. Henry with Stevenson.

There are letters of O. Henry's telling of his first experiences with "the editor fellers" and recent book reports which show that the public has bought seven hundred and fifty thousand copies of his books in twelve months, and that two of his stories have been put on the stage and many of them dramatized for the "movies."

But in all the material, reports, biographical sketches, and so forth, the most revealing things are his own letters. Almost always they are filled with quaint conceits, usually with a kind of cartoon humour and sometimes with puns. They show little scholarship but much humanity. They are the kind of letters that give the most pleasure to an average person.

In the last years of his life Sydney Porter was never well and he constantly referred to his ill health in his letters, but always with good humour and good cheer.

For instance, he wrote in a letter to his publishers:

My Dear Lanier:

In a short time, say two weeks at the outside, I'll turn in enough of the book for the purposes you require, as per your recent letter.

I've been pretty well handicapped for a couple of months and am in the hands of a fine tyrant of a doctor, who makes me come to see him every other day, and who has forbidden me to leave the city until he is through with me, and then only under his own auspices and direction. It seems that the goddess Hygiene and I have been strangers for years; and now Science must step in and repair the damage. My doctor is a miracle worker and promises that in a few weeks he will double my capacity, which sounds very good both for me and for him, when the payment of the bill is considered.

Later he wrote Mr. Steger from Asheville:

Dear Colonel Steger:

I'd have answered your letter, but I've been under the weather with a slight relapse. But on the whole I'm improving vastly. I've a doctor who says I've absolutely no physical trouble except neurasthenia, and that outdoor exercise and air will fix me as good as new. As for the diagnoses of the New York doctors—they are absolutely without foundation. I am twenty pounds lighter and can climb mountains like a goat.

Some time previous to this he wrote in a similar vein to a New York editor:

My Dear Colonel:

I've been intending to write you a long time, but the fact is, I haven't written a line of MS. and scarcely a letter since I've been down here. I've been putting in all my time trying to get back in good shape again. The simple life has been the thing I needed, and by or before Christmas I expect to be at work again in better condition than ever. It is lonesome down here as Broadway when you are broke, but I shall try to stick it out a couple of weeks or so longer.

Tell *Hampton's* not to get discouraged about their story. It'll come pretty soon, and be all the better for the wait. As I said, I haven't sent out a line since I've been here—haven't earned a cent; just lived on nerve and persimmons.

Hope you'll get your project through all right, and make a million. With the same old fraternal and nocturnal regards, I remain,

Yours as usual,

S. P.

His ill health kept him from writing either much or regularly, and consequently he was often temporarily out of money in spite of the fact that his stories were in great demand. To the same editor to whom he wrote of his health at another time he sent this typical letter concerning finances.

The Caledonia.

MY DEAR COLONEL GRIFFITH:

If you've got $100 right in your desk drawer you can have my next story, which will be ready next Tuesday at the latest. That will pay half. The other half on delivery.

I'm always wanting money, and I have to have a century this morning.

I just wanted to give you a chance at the story *at summer rates*, if you want it.

Please give the bearer a positive answer, as I'll have to know at once so as to place it elsewhere this forenoon.

Yours very truly,
SYDNEY PORTER.

P.S.—Story guaranteed satisfactory or another supplied.

This letter was written when his stories were in great demand, when he could sell many more than he could write, and sell them at higher prices than this letter indicates. Not ten years before that, however, he was unknown to the magazine field of literature.

About the time that he succeeded in selling his first stories to *Everybody's* he began a correspondence with an old friend, A. J. Jennings, ex-train robber, lawyer, author, and reformer, which contains the history of the now famous story Holding Up a Train.* The first letter was as follows:

DEAR JENNINGS:

I have intended to write you and Billy every week since I left, but kept postponing it because I expect to move on to Washington (sounds like Stonewall Jackson talk, doesn't it?) almost any time. I am very comfortably situated here, but expect to leave in a couple of weeks anyhow.

I have been doing quite a deal of business with the editors since I got down to work, and have made more than I could at any other business.

Special regards to "Tex." Love to Hans and Fritz.

Sincerely yours,
W. S. P.

* See "Sixes and Sevens."

This letter suggested the idea which was later worked out between them, Jennings supplying the data and Porter putting on the finishing touches. In a second letter [included in the Letters already published in "Rolling Stones"] O. Henry explained how the article ought to be written. A part of this letter might well be in every beginner's scrapbook, for there was never better advice about writing: "Begin abruptly without any philosophizing" is part of his doctrine. I know of one magazine office where they take out the first paragraph of at least a third of the articles that are accepted for the simple reason that they do not add anything to the story. These first paragraphs bear the same relation to progress in the story as cranking an automobile does to progress on the road. They are merely to get the engine running.

"Describe the facts and details—information is what we want—the main idea is to be natural, direct, and concise." It would be hard to get better advice than this.

In the spirit of these later letters and in their style there is little to distinguish them from the epistles he sent back to North Carolina when he first went to Texas, except the difference in length. This letter to Mrs. Hall, the mother of the men on whose ranch Porter lived, is a fair sample of these early writings.

La Salle Co., Texas.

DEAR MRS. HALL:

Your welcome letter, which I received a good while

ago, was much appreciated, and I thought I would answer it in the hopes of getting another from you. I am very short of news, so if you find anything in this letter rather incredible, get Dr. Beall to discount it for you to the proper size. He always questions my veracity since I came out here. Why didn't he do it when I was at home? Dick has got his new house done, and it looks very comfortable and magnificent. It has a tobacco-barn-like grandeur about it that always strikes a stranger with awe, and during a strong north wind the safest place about it is outside at the northern end.

A coloured lady is now slinging hash in the kitchen and has such an air of command and condescension about her that the pots and kettles all get out of her way with a rush. I think she is a countess or a dukess in disguise. Catulla has grown wonderfully since you left; thirty or forty new houses have gone up and thirty or forty barrels of whiskey gone down. The bar-keeper is going to Europe on a tour next summer and is thinking of buying Mexico for his little boy to play with. They are getting along finely with the pasture; there are sixty or seventy men at work on the fence and have been having good weather for working. Ed. Brockman is there in charge of the commissary tent, and issues provisions to the contractors. I saw him last week, and he seemed very well.

Lee came up and asked me to go down to the camps and take Brockman's place for a week or so while he went to San Antonio. Well, I went down some six or seven miles from the ranch. On arriving I counted at the commissary tent nine niggers, sixteen Mexicans, seven hounds, twenty-one six-shooters, four desperadoes, three shotguns, and a barrel of molasses. Inside there were a good many sacks of corn, flour, meal, sugar, beans, coffee, and potatoes, a big box of bacon, some boots, shoes, clothes, saddles, rifles, tobacco, and some more hounds. The work was to issue the stores to the contractors as they sent for them, and was light and easy to do. Out at the rear of the tent they had started a graveyard of men who had either kicked one of the hounds or prophesied a norther. When night came, the gentleman whose good fortune it was to be dispensing the stores gathered up his saddle-blankets, four old corn sacks, an oil coat and a sheep skin, made all the room he could in the tent by shifting and arranging the bacon, meal, etc., gave a sad look at the dogs that immediately filled the vacuum, and went and slept outdoors. The few days I was there I was treated more as a guest than one doomed to labour. Had an offer to gamble from the nigger cook, and was allowed as an especial favour to drive up the nice, pretty horses and give them some corn. And the kind of accommodating old tramps and cowboys that constitute the outfit would drop in and board, and sleep and smoke, and cuss and gamble, and lie and brag, and do everything in their power to make the time pass pleasantly and profitably —to themselves. I enjoyed the thing very much, and one evening when I saw Brockman roll up to the camp, I was very sorry, and went off very early next morning in order to escape the heartbreaking sorrow of parting and leave-taking with the layout.

Now, if you think this fine letter worth a reply, write me a long letter and tell me what I would like to know, and I will rise up and call you a friend in need, and send you a fine cameria obscuria view of this ranch and itemized account of its operations and manifold charms. Tell Dr. Beall not to send me any cake, it would make some postmaster on the road ill if he should eat too much, and I am a friend to all humanity. I am writing by a very poor light, which must excuse bad spelling and uninteresting remarks.

I remain,
Very respectfully yours,
W. S. PORTER.

Everybody well.

More interesting, however, than these early Texas letters in showing the spirit of the man are the letters that he wrote from time to time to his daughter, Margaret, especially those written when she was a little girl. In them he speaks quite often of Uncle Remus, which they evidently read together, and they are all filled with the quaint conceits that enliven the two following:

MY DEAR MARGARET:

I ought to have answered your last letter sooner, but I haven't had a chance. It's getting mighty cool now. It won't be long before persimmons are ripe in Tennessee. I don't think you ever ate any persimmons, did you? I think persimmons pudden (not pudding) is better than cantalope or watermelon either. If you stay until they get ripe you must get somebody to make you one.

If it snows while you are there, you must try some fried snowballs, too. They are mighty good with Jack Frost gravy.

You must see how big and fat you can get before you go back to Austin.

When I come home I want to find you big and strong enough to pull me all about town on a sled when we

have a snow storm. Won't that be nice? I just
thought I'd write this little letter in a hurry so the
postman would get it, and when I'm in a hurry I never
can think of anything to write about. You and
Mummy must have a good time, and keep a good lookout and don't let tramps or yellowjackets catch you.
I'll try to write something better next time. Write
soon.

Your loving
PAPA.

February 14, 1900.

DEAR MARGARET:

It has been quite a long time since I heard from you.
I got a letter from you in the last century, and a letter
once very hundred years is not very often. I have been
waiting from day to day, putting off writing to you, as
I have been expecting to have something to send you,
but it hasn't come yet, and I thought I would write
anyhow.

I hope your watch runs all right. When you write
again be sure and look at it and tell me what time it
is, so I won't have to get up and look at the clock.

With much love,
PAPA.

As the last of these little sidelights on his character
and humour which these letters convey it is fitting to
give two showing a peculiarly strong trait—his modesty. He did not seek publicity for himself and he
had a lower opinion of his work as work that would
last than almost any one else. He wrote in all sincerity to his publishers after the Christmas of 1908:

Little Pictures of O. Henry

January 1, 1909.

My Dear Mr. Lanier:

I want to say how very much I admire and appreciate the splendid edition of my poor stories that you all put in my stocking for Christmas. Unworthy though they were for such a dress, they take on from it such an added importance that I am sure they will stimulate me to do something worthy of such a binding.

I would say by all means don't let the Lipton Pub. Co. escape. Wine 'em or chase 'em in an auto and sell 'em all the "Pancakes" they can eat. Any little drippings of Maple Syrup will come in handy after the havoc of Christmas.

I'll leave things of this sort freely to your judgment. A Happy New Year to yourself and the House

Very truly yours,

SYDNEY PORTER.

To an admirer who asked for his picture for publication he jocularly refused a request which to most authors is merely a business opportunity. It is a characteristic letter. It was not until very shortly before his death that through much persuasion Sydney Porter finally allowed himself, his picture, and O. Henry to be identified together.

My Dear Mr. Hannigan:

Your letter through McClures' received. Your brief submitted (in re photo) is so flattering that I almost regret being a modest man. I have had none taken for several years except one, which was secured against my wishes and printed by a magazine. I haven't even one in my own possession. I don't believe in inflicting one's picture on the public unless one has done something to justify it—and I never take Peruna.

Sorry! you'd get one if I had it.

That lunch proposition sounds all right—may be in Boston some time and need it.

With regards,

Yours truly,
O. HENRY.

THE KNIGHT IN DISGUISE *

CONCERNING O. HENRY (SYDNEY PORTER)

By Nicholas Vachel Lindsay

Is THIS Sir Philip Sidney, this loud clown,
The darling of the glad and gaping town?
This is that dubious hero of the press
Whose slangy tongue and insolent address
Were spiced to rouse on Sunday afternoon
The man with yellow journals round him strewn.
We laughed and dozed, then roused and read again
And vowed O. Henry funniest of men.
He always worked a triple-hinged surprise
To end the scene and make one rub his eyes.

He comes with vaudeville, with stare and leer.
He comes with megaphone and specious cheer.
His troup, too fat or short or long or lean,
Step from the pages of the magazine
With slapstick or sombrero or with cane:
The rube, the cowboy, or the masher vain.

* This poem is reprinted with one or two slight changes which we make at the author's request, from "General William Booth Enters into Heaven, and Other Poems," by Nicholas Vachel Lindsay, published in 1916 by the Macmillan Company.

They overact each part. But at the height
Of banter and of canter, and delight
The masks fall off for one queer instant there
And show real faces; faces full of care
And desperate longing; love that's hot or cold;
And subtle thoughts, and countenances bold.
The masks go back. 'Tis one more joke.
   Laugh on!
The goodly grown-up company is gone.

No doubt, had he occasion to address
The brilliant court of purple-clad Queen Bess,
He would have wrought for them the best he knew
And led more loftily his actor-crew.
How coolly he misquoted. 'Twas his art—
Slave-scholar, who misquoted—from the heart.
So when we slapped his back with friendly roar
Esop awaited him without the door,—
Esop the Greek, who made dull masters laugh
With little tales of *fox* and *dog* and *calf*.

And be it said, amid his pranks so odd
With something nigh to chivalry he trod—
The fragile drear and driven would defend—
The little shop-girls' knight unto the end.
Yea, he had passed, ere we could understand
The blade of Sidney glimmered in his hand.
Yea, ere we knew, Sir Philip's sword was drawn
With valiant cut and thrust, and he was gone.

THE AMAZING GENIUS OF O. HENRY *
By Stephen Leacock

TO BRITISH readers of this book the above heading may look like the title of a comic story of Irish life with the apostrophe gone wrong. It is, alas! only too likely that many, perhaps the majority, of British readers have never heard of O. Henry. It is quite possible also that they are not ashamed of themselves on that account. Such readers would, in truly British fashion, merely classify O. Henry as one of the people that "one has never heard of." If there was any disparagement implied, it would be, as O. Henry himself would have remarked, "on him." And yet there have been sold in the United States, so it is claimed, one million copies of his books.

The point is one which illustrates some of the difficulties which beset the circulation of literature, though written in a common tongue, to and fro across the Atlantic. The British and the American public has each its own preconceived ideas about what it proposes to like. The British reader turns with distaste from anything which bears to him the taint of literary vul-

* From "Essays and Literary Studies," 1916, John Lane Co.

garity or cheapness; he instinctively loves anything which seems to have the stamp of scholarship and revels in a classical allusion even when he doesn't understand it.

This state of mind has its qualities and its defects. Undoubtedly it makes for the preservation of a standard and a proper appreciation of the literature of the past. It helps to keep the fool in his place, imitating, like a watchful monkey, the admirations of better men. But on its defective side it sins against the light of intellectual honesty.

The attitude of the American reading public is turned the other way. I am not speaking here of the small minority which reads Walter Pater in a soft leather cover, listens to lectures on Bergsonian illusionism and prefers a drama league to a bridge club. I refer to the great mass of the American people, such as live in frame dwellings in the country, or exist in city boarding-houses, ride in the subway, attend a ten-twenty-thirty vaudeville show in preference to an Ibsen drama, and read a one-cent newspaper because it is intellectually easier than a two. This is the real public. It is not, of course, ignorant in the balder sense. A large part of it is, technically, highly educated and absorbs the great mass of the fifty thousand college degrees granted in America each year. But it has an instinctive horror of "learning," such as a cat feels toward running water. It has invented for itself the ominous word "highbrow" as a sign of warning placed over things to be avoided. This word to the American mind conveys much the same "taboo" as haunts the tomb of a Polynesian warrior, or the sacred horror that enveloped in ancient days the dark pine grove of a sylvan deity.

For the ordinary American this word "highbrow" has been pieced together out of recollections of a college professor in a black tail coat and straw hat destroying the peace of an Adirondack boarding-house: out of the unforgotten dullness of a Chautauqua lecture course, or the expiring agonies of a Browning Society. To such a mind the word "highbrow" sweeps a wide and comprehensive area with the red flag of warning. It covers, for example, the whole of history, or, at least, the part of it antecedent to the two last presidential elections. All foreign literature, and all references to it are "highbrow." Shakespeare, except as revived at twenty-five cents a seat with proper alterations in the text, is "highbrow." The works of Milton, the theory of evolution, and, in fact, all science other than Christian science, is "highbrow." A man may only read and discuss such things at his peril. If he does so, he falls forthwith into the class of the Chautauqua lecturer and the vacation professor; he loses all claim to mingle in the main stream of life by taking a hand at ten-cent poker, or giving his views on the outcome of the 1916 elections.

All this, however, by way of preliminary discussion suggested by the strange obscurity of O. Henry in

Great Britain, and the wide and increasing popularity of his books in America. O. Henry is, more than any author who ever wrote in the United States, an American writer. As such his work may well appear to a British reader strange and unusual, and, at a casual glance, not attractive. It looks at first sight as if written in American slang, as if it were the careless, unrevised production of a journalist. But this is only the impression of an open page, or at best, a judgment formed by a reader who has had the ill-fortune to light upon the less valuable part of O. Henry's output. Let it be remembered that he wrote over two hundred stories. Even in Kentucky, where it is claimed that all whiskey is good whiskey, it is admitted that some whiskey is not so good as the rest. So it may be allowed to the most infatuated admirer of O. Henry, to admit that some of his stories are not as good as the others. Yet even that admission would be reluctant.

But let us recommence in more orthodox fashion.

O. Henry—as he signed himself—was born in 1867, most probably at Greensboro, North Carolina. For the first thirty or thirty-five years of his life, few knew or cared where he was born, or whither he was going. Now that he has been dead five years he shares already with Homer the honour of a disputed birthplace.

His real name was William Sydney Porter. His *nom de plume*, O. Henry—hopelessly tame and colourless from a literary point of view—seems to have been

The Amazing Genius of O. Henry 49

adopted in a whimsical moment, with no great thought as to its aptness. It is amazing that he should have selected so poor a pen name. Those who can remember their first shock of pleased surprise on hearing that Rudyard Kipling's name was really Rudyard Kipling, will feel something like pain in learning that any writer could deliberately christen himself "O. Henry."

The circumstance is all the more peculiar inasmuch as O. Henry's works abound in ingenious nomenclature. The names that he claps on his Central American adventurers are things of joy to the artistic eye— General Perrico Ximenes Villablanca Falcon! Ramon Angel de las Cruzes y Miraflores, president of the republic of Anchuria! Don Señor el Coronel Encarnación Rios! The very spirit of romance and revolution breathes through them! Or what more beautiful for a Nevada town than Topaz City? What name more appropriate for a commuter's suburb than Floralhurst? And these are only examples among thousands. In all the two hundred stories that O. Henry wrote, there is hardly a single name that is inappropriate or without a proper literary suggestiveness, except the name that he signed to them.

While still a boy, O. Henry (there is no use in calling him anything else) went to Texas, where he worked for three years on a ranch. He drifted into the city of Houston and got employment on a newspaper. A year later he bought a newspaper of his own in Austin,

Texas, for the sum of two hundred and fifty dollars. He rechristened it *The Rolling Stone*, wrote it, and even illustrated it, himself. But the paper was too well named. Its editor himself rolled away from it, and from the shores of Texas the wandering restlessness that was characteristic of him wafted him down the great Gulf to the enchanted land of Central America. Here he "knocked around," as he himself has put it, "mostly among refugees and consuls." Here, too, was laid the foundation of much of his most characteristic work—his "Cabbages and Kings," and such stories as Phœbe and The Fourth in Salvador.

Latin America fascinated O. Henry. The languor of the tropics; the sunlit seas with their open bays and broad sanded beaches, with green palms nodding on the slopes above—white-painted steamers lazily at anchor—quaint Spanish towns, with adobe houses and wide squares, sunk in their noon-day sleep—beautiful Señoritas drowsing away the afternoon in hammocks; the tinkling of the mule bells on the mountain track above the town—the cries of unknown birds issuing from the dense green of the unbroken jungle—and at night, in the soft darkness, the low murmur of the guitar, soft thrumming with the voice of love—these are the sights and sounds of O. Henry's Central America. Here live and move his tattered revolutionists, his gaudy generals of the mimic army of the existing republic; hither ply his white-painted steamers of the fruit trade; here the American consul, with a shadowed past and $600 a year, drinks away the remembrance of his northern energy and his college education in the land of forgetfulness. Hither the absconding banker from the States is dropped from the passing steamer, clutching tight in his shaking hand his valise of stolen dollars; him the disguised detective, lounging beside the little drinking shop, watches with a furtive eye. And here in this land of enchantment the broken lives, the wasted hopes, the ambition that was never reached, the frailty that was never conquered, are somehow pieced together and illuminated into what they might have been—and even the reckless crime and the open sin, viewed in the softened haze of such an atmosphere, are half forgiven.

Whether this is the "real Central America" or not is of no consequence. It probably is not. The "real Central America" may best be left to the up-to-date specialist, the energetic newspaper expert, or the travelling lady correspondent—to all such persons, in fact, as are capable of writing "Six Weeks in Nicaragua," or "Costa Rica as I Saw It." Most likely the Central America of O. Henry is as gloriously unreal as the London of Charles Dickens, or the Salem of Nathaniel Hawthorne, or any other beautiful picture of the higher truth of life that can be shattered into splinters in the distorting of cold fact.

From Central America O. Henry rolled, drifted or floated—there was no method in his life—back to Texas again. Here he worked for two weeks in a drugstore. This brief experience supplied him all the rest of his life with local colour and technical material for his stories.* So well has he used it that the obstinate legend still runs that O. Henry was a druggist. A strict examination of his work would show that he knew the names of about seventeen drugs and was able to describe the rolling of pills with the life-like accuracy of one who has rolled them. But it was characteristic of his instinct for literary values that even on this slender basis O. Henry was able to make his characters "take down from shelves" such mysterious things as *Sod. et Pot. Tart.* or discuss whether magnesia carbonate or pulverized glycerine is the best excipient, and in moments of high tragedy poison themselves with "tincture of aconite."

Whether these terms are correctly used or not I do not know. Nor can I conceive that it matters. O. Henry was a literary artist first, last, and always. It was the effect and the feeling that he wanted. For technical accuracy he cared not one whit. There is a certain kind of author who thinks to make literature by introducing, let us say, a plumber using seven different kinds of tap-washers with seven different names; and there is a certain type of reader who is thereby conscious of seven different kinds of ignorance and is

* As a matter of fact, he did serve as a drug clerk for a considerable period of time, when a very young man, in his uncle's drugstore in Greensboro.—ED.

The Amazing Genius of O. Henry 53

fascinated forthwith. From pedantry of this sort O. Henry is entirely free. Even literal accuracy is nothing to him so long as he gets his effect. Thus he commences one of his stories with the brazen statement: "In Texas you may journey for a thousand miles in a straight line." You can't, of course; and O. Henry knew it. It is only his way of saying that Texas is a very big place. So with his tincture of aconite. It may be poisonous or it may not be. But it sounds poisonous and that is enough for O. Henry. This is true art.

After his brief drugstore experience O. Henry moved to New Orleans. Even in his Texan and Central American days he seems to have scribbled stories. In New Orleans he set to work deliberately as a writer. Much of his best work was poured forth with prodigality of genius into the columns of the daily press without thought or fame. The money that he received, so it is said, was but a pittance. Stories that would sell to-day—were O. Henry alive and writing them now—for a thousand dollars, went for next to nothing. Throughout his life money meant little or nothing to him. If he had it, he spent it, loaned it, or gave it away. When he had it not he bargained with an editor for the payment in advance of a story which he meant to write, and of which he exhibited the title or a few sentences as a sample, and which he wrote, faithfully enough, "when he got round to it." The story runs of how one night a beggar on the street asked O. Henry for money. He drew forth a coin from his pocket in the darkness and handed it to the man. A few moments later the beggar looked at the coin under a street lamp, and, being even such a beggar as O. Henry loved to write about, he came running back with the words, "Say, you made a mistake, this is a twenty-dollar gold piece." "I know it is," said O. Henry, "but it's all I have."

The story may not be true. But at least it ought to be.

From New Orleans O. Henry moved to New York and became, for the rest of his life, a unit among the "four million" dwellers in flats and apartment houses and sandstone palaces who live within the roar of the elevated railway, and from whom the pale light of the moon and the small effects of the planetary system are overwhelmed in the glare of the Great White Way. Here O. Henry's finest work was done—inimitable, unsurpassable stories that make up the volumes entitled "The Four Million," "The Trimmed Lamp," and "The Voice of the City."

Marvellous indeed they are. Written offhand with the bold carelessness of the pen that only genius dare use, but revealing behind them such a glow of the imagination and such a depth of understanding of the human heart as only genius can make manifest.

What O. Henry did for Central America he does again for New York. It is transformed by the magic of his imagination. He waves a wand over it and it becomes a city of mystery and romance. It is no longer the roaring, surging metropolis that we thought we knew, with its clattering elevated, its unending crowds, and on every side the repellent selfishness of the rich, the grim struggle of the poor, and the listless despair of the outcast. It has become, as O. Henry loves to call it, Bagdad upon the Subway. The glare has gone. There is a soft light suffusing the city. Its corner drugstores turn to enchanted bazaars. From the open doors of its restaurants and palm rooms there issues such a melody of softened music that we feel we have but to cross the threshold and there is Bagdad waiting for us beyond. A transformed waiter hands us to a chair at a little table—Arabian, I will swear it—beside an enchanted rubber tree. There is red wine such as Omar Khayyam drank, here on Sixth Avenue. At the tables about us are a strange and interesting crew —dervishes in the disguise of American business men, caliphs masquerading as tourists, bedouins from Syria, and fierce fantassins from the desert turned into western visitors from Texas, and among them—can we believe our eyes—houris from the inner harems of Ispahan and Candahar, whom we mistook but yesterday for the ladies of a Shubert chorus! As we pass out we pay our money to an enchanted cashier with golden hair —sitting behind glass—under the spell of some magician without a doubt, and then taking O. Henry's hand we wander forth among the everchanging scenes of night adventure, the mingled tragedy and humour of The Four Million that his pen alone can depict. Nor did ever Haroun-al-Raschid and his viziers, wandering at will in the narrow streets of their Arabian city, meet such varied adventure as lies before us, strolling hand in hand with O. Henry in the new Bagdad that he reveals.

But let us turn to the stories themselves. O. Henry wrote in all two hundred short stories of an average of about fifteen pages each. This was the form in which his literary activity shaped itself by instinct. A novel he never wrote, a play he often meditated but never achieved. One of his books—"Cabbages and Kings" —can make a certain claim to be continuous. But even this is rather a collection of little stories than a single piece of fiction. But it is an error of the grossest kind to say that O. Henry's work is not sustained. In reality his canvas is vast. His New York stories, like those of Central America or of the West, form one great picture as gloriously comprehensive in its scope as the lengthiest novels of a Dickens or the canvas of a Da Vinci. It is only the method that is different, not the result.

It is hard indeed to illustrate O. Henry's genius by the quotation of single phrases and sentences. The humour that is in his work lies too deep for that. His is not the comic wit that explodes the reader into a huge guffaw of laughter and vanishes. His humour is of that deep quality that smiles at life itself and mingles our amusement with our tears.

Still harder is it to try to show the amazing genius of O. Henry as a "plot maker," as a designer of incident. No one better than he can hold the reader in suspense. Nay, more than that, the reader scarcely knows that he is "suspended," until at the very close of the story O. Henry, so to speak, turns on the lights and the whole tale is revealed as an entirety. But to do justice to a plot in a few paragraphs is almost impossible. Let the reader consider to what a few poor shreds even the best of our novels or plays is reduced, when we try to set forth the basis of it in the condensed phrase of a text-book of literature, or diminish it to the language of the "scenario" of a moving picture. Let us take an example.

We will transcribe our immortal "Hamlet" as faithfully as we can into a few words with an eye to explain the plot and nothing else. It will run about as follows:

"Hamlet's uncle kills his father and marries his mother, and Hamlet is so disturbed about this that he either is mad or pretends to be mad. In this condition he drives his sweetheart insane and she drowns, or practically drowns, herself. Hamlet then kills his uncle's chief adviser behind an arras either in mistake for a rat, or not. Hamlet then gives poison to his uncle and his mother, stabs Laertes and kills himself. There is much discussion among the critics as to whether his actions justify us in calling him insane."

There! The example is, perhaps, not altogether convincing. It does not seem somehow, faithful though it is, to do Shakespeare justice. But let it at least illustrate the point under discussion. The mere bones of a plot are nothing. We could scarcely form a judgment on female beauty by studying the skeletons of a museum of anatomy.

But with this distinct understanding, let me try to present the outline of a typical O. Henry story. I select it from the volume entitled "The Gentle Grafter," a book that is mainly concerned with the wiles of Jeff Peters and his partners and associates. Mr. Peters, who acts as the narrator of most of the stories, typifies the perennial fakir and itinerant grafter of the Western States—ready to turn his hand to anything from selling patent medicines under a naphtha lamp on the street corner of a Western town to peddling bargain Bibles from farm to farm—anything, in short, that does not involve work and carries with it the peculiar excitement of trying to keep out of the State penitentiary. All the world loves a grafter—at least a genial and ingenious grafter—a Robin Hood who plunders an abbot to feed a beggar, an Alfred Jingle, a Scapin, a Raffles, or any of the multifarious characters of the world's literature who reveal the fact that much that is best in humanity may flourish even on the shadowy side of technical iniquity. Of this glorious company is Mr. Jefferson Peters. But let us take him as he is revealed in "Jeff Peters as a Personal Magnet" and let us allow him to introduce himself and his business.

"I struck Fisher Hill," Mr. Peters relates, "in a buckskin suit, moccasins, long hair, and a thirty-carat diamond ring that I got from an actor in Texarkana. I don't know what he ever did with the pocket-knife I swapped him for it.

"I was Dr. Waugh-hoo, the celebrated Indian medicine man. I carried only one best bet just then, and that was Resurrection Bitters. It was made of lifegiving plants and herbs accidentally discovered by Ta-qua-la, the beautiful wife of the chief of the Choctaw Nation, while gathering truck to garnish a platter of boiled dog for an annual corn dance. . . ." In the capacity of Dr. Waugh-hoo, Mr. Peters "struck Fisher Hill." He went to a druggist and got credit for half a gross of eight-ounce bottles and corks, and with the help of the running water from the tap in the hotel room, he spent a long evening manufacturing Resurrection Bitters. The next evening the sales began. The bitters at fifty cents a bottle "started off like sweetbreads on toast at a vegetarian dinner." Then there intervenes a constable with a German silver badge. "Have you got a city license?" he asks, and Mr. Peters's medicinal activity comes to a full stop. The threat of prosecution under the law for practising medicine without a license puts Mr. Peters for the moment out of business.

He returns sadly to his hotel, pondering on his next

move. Here by good fortune he meets a former acquaintance, a certain Andy Tucker, who has just finished a tour in the Southern States, working the Great Cupid Combination Package on the chivalrous and unsuspecting South.

"Andy," says Jeff, in speaking of his friend's credentials, "was a good street man: and he was more than that—he respected his profession and was satisfied with 300 per cent. profit. He had plenty of offers to go into the illegitimate drug and garden seed business, but he was never to be tempted off the straight path."

Andy and Jeff take counsel together in long debate on the porch of the hotel.

And here, apparently, a piece of good luck came to Jeff's help. The very next morning a messenger brings word that the Mayor of the town is suddenly taken ill. The only doctor of the place is twenty miles away. Jeff Peters is summoned to the Mayor's bedside. . . . "This Mayor Banks," Jeff relates, "was in bed all but his whiskers and feet. He was making internal noises that would have had everybody in San Francisco hiking for the parks. A young man was standing by the bedside holding a cup of water. . . ." Mr. Peters, called to the patient's side, is very cautious. He draws attention to the fact that he is not a qualified practitioner, is not "a regular disciple of S. Q. Lapius."

The Mayor groans in pain. The young man at the bedside, introduced as Mr. Biddle, the Mayor's nephew, urges Mr. Peters—or Doctor Waugh-hoo—in the name of common humanity to attempt a cure.

Finally Jeff Peters promises to treat the Mayor by "scientific demonstration." He proposes, he says, to make use of the "great doctrine of psychic financiering —of the enlightening school of long-distance subconscious treatment of fallacies and meningitis—of that wonderful indoor sport known as personal magnetism." But he warns the Mayor that the treatment is difficult. It uses up great quantities of soul strength. It comes high. It cannot be attempted under two hundred and fifty dollars.

The Mayor groans. But he yields. The treatment begins.

"You ain't sick," says Dr. Waugh-hoo, looking the patient right in the eye. "You ain't got any pain. The right lobe of your perihelion is subsided."

The result is surprising. The Mayor's system seems to respond at once. "I do feel some better, Doc," he says, "darned if I don't."

Mr. Peters assumes a triumphant air. He promises to return next day for a second and final treatment.

"I'll come back," he says to the young man, "at eleven. You may give him eight drops of turpentine and three pounds of steak. Good-morning."

Next day the final treatment is given. The Mayor is completely restored. Two hundred and fifty dollars, all in cash, is handed to "Dr. Waugh-hoo." The young man asks for a receipt. It is no sooner written out by Jeff Peters, than:

" 'Now do your duty, officer,' says the Mayor, grinning much unlike a sick man.

"Mr. Biddle lays his hand on my arm.

" 'You're under arrest, Dr. Waugh-hoo, alias Peters,' says he, 'for practising medicine without authority under the State law.'

" 'Who are you?' I asks.

" 'I'll tell you who he is,' says Mr. Mayor, sitting up in bed. 'He's a detective employed by the State Medical Society. He's been following you over five counties. He came to me yesterday and we fixed up this scheme to catch you. I guess you won't do any more doctoring around these parts, Mr. Fakir. What was it you said I had, Doc?' the Mayor laughs, 'compound—well, it wasn't softening of the brain, I guess, anyway.' "

Ingenious, isn't it? One hadn't suspected it. But let the reader kindly note the conclusion of the story as it follows, handled with the lightning rapidity of a conjuring trick.

" 'Come on, officer,' says I, dignified. 'I may as well make the best of it.' And then I turns to old Banks and rattles my chains.

" 'Mr. Mayor,' says I, 'the time will come soon when you'll believe that personal magnetism is a success. And you'll be sure that it succeeded in this case, too.'

"And I guess it did.

"When we got nearly to the gate, I says: 'We might meet somebody now, Andy. I reckon you better take 'em off, and——' Hey? Why, of course it was Andy Tucker. That was his scheme; and that's how we got the capital to go into business together."

Now let us set beside this a story of a different type, The Furnished Room, which appears in the volume called "The Four Million." It shows O. Henry at his best as a master of that supreme pathos that springs, with but little adventitious aid of time or circumstance, from the fundamental things of life itself. In the sheer art of narration there is nothing done by Maupassant that surpasses The Furnished Room. The story runs —so far as one dare attempt to reproduce it without quoting it all word for word—after this fashion.

The scene is laid in New York in the lost district of the lower West Side, where the wandering feet of actors and one-week transients seek furnished rooms in dilapidated houses of fallen grandeur.

One evening after dark a young man prowled among these crumbling red mansions, ringing their bells. At the twelfth he rested his lean hand-baggage upon the step and wiped the dust from his hatband and forehead. The bell sounded faint and far away in some remote hollow depths. . . . "I have the third floor

back vacant since a week back," says the landlady.
. . . "It's a nice room. It ain't often vacant. I had
some most elegant people in it last summer—no trouble
at all and paid in advance to the minute. The water's
at the end of the hall. Sprowls and Mooney kept it
three months. They done a vaudeville sketch. Miss
B'retta Sprowls, you may have heard of her—Oh, that
was just the stage name—right there over the dresser is
where the marriage certificate hung, framed. The gas
is here and you see there's plenty of closet room. It's a
room every one likes. It never stays idle long——"

The young man takes the room, paying a week in
advance. Then he asks:

"A young girl—Miss Vashner—Miss Eloise Vashner—do you remember such a one among your lodgers?
She would be singing on the stage most likely."

The landlady shakes her head. They comes and
goes, she tells him, she doesn't call that one to mind.

It is the same answer that he has been receiving, up
and down, in the crumbling houses of the lost district,
through weeks and months of wandering. No, always no. Five months of ceaseless interrogation and
the inevitable negative. So much time spent by day
in questioning managers, agents, schools, and choruses;
by night among the audiences of theatres from all-star
casts down to music halls so low that he dreaded to
find what he most hoped for. . . . The young man
left in his sordid room of the third floor back, among
its decayed furniture, its ragged brocade upholstery,

sinks into a chair. The dead weight of despair is on him. . . . Then, suddenly, as he rested there, the room was filled with the strong, sweet odour of mignonette—the flower that she had always loved, the perfume that she had always worn. It is as if her very presence was beside him in the empty room. He rises. He cries aloud, "What, dear?" as if she had called to him. She has been there in the room. He knows it. He feels it. Then eager, tremulous with hope, he searches the room, tears open the crazy chest of drawers, fumbles upon the shelves, for some sign of her. Nothing and still nothing—a crumpled playbill, a half-smoked cigar, the dreary and ignoble small records of many a peripatetic tenant, but of the woman that he seeks, nothing. Yet still that haunting perfume that seems to speak her presence at his very side.

The young man dashes trembling from the room. Again he questions the landlady—was there not, before him in the room, a young lady? Surely there must have been—fair, of medium height, and with reddish gold hair? Surely there was?

But the landlady, as if obdurate, shakes her head. "I can tell you again," she says, " 'twas Sprowls and Mooney, as I said. Miss B'retta Sprowls, it was, in the theatres, but Missis Mooney she was. The marriage certificate hung, framed, on a nail over——"

. . . The young man returns to his room. It is all over. His search in vain. The ebbing of his last hope has drained his faith. . . . For a time he sat staring at the yellow, singing gaslight. Then he rose. He walked to the bed and began to tear the sheets into strips. With the blade of his knife he drove them tightly into every crevice around windows and door. When all was snug and taut he turned out the light, turned the gas full on again, and laid himself gratefully upon the bed.

And now let the reader note the ending paragraphs of the story, so told that not one word of it must be altered or abridged from the form in which O. Henry framed it.

It was Mrs. McCool's night to go with the can for beer. So she fetched it and sat with Mrs. Purdy (the landlady) in one of those subterranean retreats where housekeepers foregather and the worm dieth seldom.

"I rented out my third floor, back, this evening," said Mrs. Purdy, across a fine circle of foam. "A young man took it. He went up to bed two hours ago."

"Now, did ye, Mrs. Purdy, ma'am!" said Mrs. McCool with intense admiration. "You do be a wonder for rentin' rooms of that kind. And did ye tell him, then?" she concluded in a husky whisper laden with mystery.

"Rooms," said Mrs. Purdy, in her furriest tones, "are furnished for to rent. I did not tell him, Mrs. McCool."

" 'Tis right ye are, ma'am; 'tis by renting rooms we

The Amazing Genius of O. Henry 67

kape alive. Ye have the rale sense for business, ma'am. There be many people will rayjict the rentin' of a room if they be tould a suicide has been after dyin' in the bed of it."

"As you say, we has our living to be making," remarked Mrs. Purdy.

"Yis, ma'am; 'tis true. 'Tis just one wake ago this day I helped ye lay out the third floor back. A pretty slip of a colleen she was to be killin' herself wid the gas—a swate little face she had, Mrs. Purdy, ma'am."

"She'd a-been called handsome, as you say," said Mrs. Purdy, assenting but critical, "but for that mole she had a-growin' by her left eyebrow. Do fill up your glass again, Mrs. McCool."

Beyond these two stories I do not care to go. But if the reader is not satisfied let him procure for himself the story called A Municipal Report in the volume "Strictly Business." After he has read it he will either pronounce O. Henry one of the greatest masters of modern fiction or else—well, or else he is a jackass. Let us put it that way.

O. Henry lived some nine years in New York but little known to the public at large. Toward the end there came to him success, a competence, and something that might be called celebrity if not fame. But it was marvellous how his light remained hid. The time came when the best known magazines eagerly sought his work. He could have commanded his own price. But the notoriety of noisy success, the personal triumph of literary conspicuousness he neither achieved nor envied. A certain cruel experience of his earlier days—tragic, unmerited, and not here to be recorded—had left him shy of mankind at large and, in the personal sense, anxious only for obscurity. Even when the American public in tens and hundreds of thousands read his matchless stories, they read them, so to speak, in isolated fashion, as personal discoveries, unaware for years of the collective greatness of O. Henry's work viewed as a total. The few who were privileged to know him seem to have valued him beyond all others and to have found him even greater than his work. And then, in mid-career as it seemed, there was laid upon him the hand of a wasting and mortal disease, which brought him slowly to his end, his courage and his gentle kindliness unbroken to the last. "I shall die," he said one winter with one of the quoted phrases that fell so aptly from his lips, "in the good old summer time." And "in the good old summer time" with a smile and a jest upon his lips he died. "Don't turn down the light," he is reported to have said to those beside his bed, and then, as the words of a popular song flickered across his mind, he added, "I'm afraid to go home in the dark."

That was in the summer of 1910. Since his death, his fame in America has grown greater and greater with every year. The laurel wreath that should have crowned his brow is exchanged for the garland laid upon his grave. And the time is coming, let us hope, when the whole English-speaking world will recognize in O. Henry one of the great masters of modern literature.

O. HENRY: AN ENGLISH VIEW

By A. St. John Adcock

USUALLY, when we write of how the critics and the public of an earlier generation were slow to recognize the genius of Meredith or Mark Rutherford, we do it with an air of severe self-righteousness which covers an implication that we in our more enlightened age are not likely to repeat such blunders, that the general taste and critical acumen of our time may safely be relied upon to assess contemporary authors at their true value and put them, with unerring promptitude, into their proper places. The fact is, of course, that even our modern literary judgments are not infallible, and that we are really in no position at all to throw stones at our forefathers. It were sufficient for us if we devoted our energies to getting the beam out of our own eye and left the dead past to bury its dead mistakes.

Take the very modern instance of O. Henry. Thousands of us are reading his stories at present and realizing with astonishment that he was a great literary artist—with astonishment because, though we are only just arriving at this knowledge of him, we learn that he commenced to write before the end of last century, and has been five years dead. Even in America, where he belonged, recognition came to him slowly; it was only toward the close of his life that he began to be counted as anything more than a popular magazine author; but now, in the States, they have sold more than a million copies of his books. His publishers announce in their advertisements that "up goes the sale of O. Henry, higher and higher every day," that he has "beaten the world record for the sale of short stories"; and the critics compete with each other in comparing him to Poe and Bret Harte, to Mark Twain and Dickens, to de Maupassant and Kipling. We cannot put ourselves right by saying that he was an American, for in the last few years at least two attempts have been made to introduce him to English readers, and both of them failed. Then a little while ago Mr. Eveleigh Nash embarked on a third attempt and commenced the publication of a uniform edition of the works of O. Henry in twelve three-and-sixpenny volumes. They hung fire a little at first, I believe, but by degrees made headway, and before the series was completed it had achieved a large and increasing success. This was recently followed by an announcement of the issue of the twelve volumes in a shilling edition by Messrs. Hodder & Stoughton; the first six have appeared, and the remainder are to be published before the end of the year, and as the publishers estimate that by then, at the present rate of sale, at least half a million copies will have been sold, one may take it that, at long last,

O. Henry is triumphantly entering into his kingdom.

In a brilliant appreciation of The Amazing Genius of O. Henry,* in his new book, "Essays and Literary Studies" (John Lane), Professor Stephen Leacock speaks of the wide and increasing popularity of O. Henry in America, and of his "strange obscurity" in Great Britain. He thinks it "only too likely that many, perhaps the majority, of British readers have never heard of O. Henry." That was certainly true when it was written, but in the last six months our long-suffering public has risen above the reproach. Professor Leacock tries to suggest a reason for our indifference. "The British reader turns with distaste," he says, "from anything which bears to him the taint of literary vulgarity or cheapness; he instinctively loves anything which seems to have the stamp of scholarship, and revels in a classical allusion even when he doesn't understand it." But for the sting in its tail and the passage that succeeds it, I should suspect this sentence of irony, for the British reader received at once and with open arms the joyous extravagances of Max Adeler (who, by the way, should not have been entirely ignored in Professor Leacock's essay on "American Humour"), and there is nothing in "Elbow Room" or "Out of the Hurly-Burly" that is funnier or more quaintly humorous than some of Henry's stories. But O. Henry can move you to tears as well as to laughter— you have not finished with him when you have called

* Reprinted in this volume, pp. 171–195.

him a humourist. He has all the gifts of the supreme teller of tales, is master of tragedy as well as of burlesque, of comedy and of romance, of the domestic and the mystery-tale of common life, and has a delicate skill in stories of the supernatural. Through every change of his theme runs a broad, genial understanding of all sorts of humanity, and his familiar, sometimes casually conversational style conceals a finished narrative art that amply justifies Professor Leacock in naming him "one of the great masters of modern literature." He is not, then, of that cheap type of author from whom, as the Professor says, the British reader "turns with distaste." He has not been received among us sooner simply because, to repeat Mr. Leacock's statement, "the majority of British readers have never heard of O. Henry," and obviously until they have heard of him it is impossible that they should read him. Therefore, the blame for our not sooner appreciating him rests, not on our general public, but on our critics and publishers. If he had been adequately published, and adequately reviewed over here before, British readers must have heard of him, and their complete vindication lies in the fact that now, when at length he has been adequately published and reviewed and so brought to their notice, they are reading his books as fast as they can lay hands on them. . . .

The life he lived was the life that was best for him. Every phase of it had its share in making him the prose troubadour that he became. Half his books are filled with stories that are shaped and coloured by his roamings, and the other half with stories that he gathered in the busy ways and, particularly, in the byways of—"Little Old New York." For the scenes, incidents, and characters of his tales he had not need to travel far outside the range of his own experiences, and it is probably this that helps to give them the carelessly intimate air of reality that is part of their strength. He touches in his descriptions lightly and swiftly, yet whether he is telling of the old-world quaintness of North Carolina, the rough lawlessness of Texas, the strange glamour of New Orleans, the slumberous, bizarre charm of obscure South American coast towns, or the noise and bustle and squalor and up-to-date magnificence of New York, his stories are steeped in colour and atmosphere. You come to think of his men and women less as characters he has drawn than as people he has known, he writes of them with such familiar acquaintance, and makes them so vividly actual to you. He is as sure and as cunning in the presentment of his exquisite señoritas, his faded, dignified Spanish grandees and planters and traders and picturesque rather comic-opera Presidents of small South American republics, as in drawing his wonderful gallery of Bowery boys, financiers, clerks, shop-girls, workers, and New York aristocrats. You scarcely realize them as creations, they seem to walk into his pages without effort. His women are, at least, as varied in type and as intensely human as his men:

he wins your sympathy for Isabel Guilbert,* who was "Eve after the fall but before the bitterness of it was felt," who "wore life as a rose in her bosom," and who, according to Keogh, could "look at a man once, and he'll turn monkey and climb trees to pick cocoanuts for her," no less than he wins it for Norah, the self-sacrificing little sewing-girl, of Blind Man's Holiday,† or the practical, loyally passionate wife, Santa Yeager, of Hearts and Crosses,‡ or the delightful Mrs. Cassidy who accepts the blows of her drunken husband as proof of his love ("Who else has got a right to be beat? I'd just like to catch him once beating anybody else!") in A Harlem Tragedy,§ which would be grotesquely farcical if it were not for its droll air of truth and the curious sense of pathos that underlies it. . . .

I am not going to attempt to say which is the best of his tales; they vary so widely in subject and manner that it is impossible to compare them. There were moods in which he saw New York in all its solid, material, commonplace realism, and moods in which it became to him "Bagdad-on-the-Subway," and was full of romance, as Soho is in Stevenson's "New Arabian Nights." His Wild West stories are a subtle blend of humour, pathos, and picturesqueness; some of his town and country stories delight you by their homely nat-

* See "Cabbages and Kings."
† See "Whirligigs."
‡ See "Heart of the West."
§ See "The Trimmed Lamp."

uralness, others are alive with sensation and excitement, others again are pure fantasy or things for nothing but laughter. Then there are such as "Roads of Destiny," which, with a strange dream-like quality, a haunting, imaginative suggestiveness, unfolds three stories of the same man—as one might see them in prevision—showing that whichever way of life he had chosen he would have been brought to the same appointed end. The eerie touch of other-world influences is upon you in this, as it is in The Door of Unrest,* an uncanny, queerly humorous legend of the Wandering Jew in a modern American city; and as it is in The Furnished Room,† which Professor Leacock justly singles out as one of the finest of O. Henry's works. "It shows O. Henry at his best," he says, "as a master of that supreme pathos that springs, with but little adventitious aid of time or circumstance, from the fundamental things of life itself. In the sheer art of narration there is nothing done by Maupassant that surpasses The Furnished Room." It could only be misrepresented in a summary, for though O. Henry always has a good story to tell, its effectiveness is always heightened immeasurably by his manner of telling it.

It is in sheer art of narration, and in the breadth and depth of his knowledge of humanity and his sympathy with it that he chiefly excels. He was too big a man to be nothing but an artist, and the bigger

* See "Sixes and Sevens."
† See "The Four Million."

artist for that reason. He has none of the conscious stylist's elaborate little tricks with words, for he is a master of language and not its slave. He is as happily colloquial as Kipling was in his early tales, but his style is as individual, as naturally his own, as a man's voice may be. He seems to go as he pleases, writing apparently just whatever words happen to be in the ink, yet all the while he is getting hold of his reader's interest, subtly shaping his narrative with the storyteller's unerring instinct, generally allowing you no glimpse of its culminating point until you are right on it. "The art of narrative," said Keogh, in "Cabbages and Kings," "consists in concealing from your audience everything it wants to know until after you expose your favourite opinions on topics foreign to the subject. A good story is like a bitter pill with the sugar coating inside of it"; and this art O. Henry practises with a skill that is invariably admirable and at times startling. More than once he leads you deftly on till you arrive at what would seem an ingenious ending, then in a sudden paragraph he will give the whole thing a quick turn and land you in a still more ingenious climax that leaves victory in the hands of the character who had seemed to have lost.

"Cabbages and Kings," a series of stories held together by a central thread of interest, is the nearest O. Henry came to writing a novel. Toward the end of his career his publishers urged him to write one and among his papers after his death was found an unfinished reply to them setting out something of his idea of the novel he would like to attempt. It was to be the story of an individual, not of a type—"the *true* record of a man's thoughts, his descriptions of his mischances and adventures, his *true* opinions of life as he has seen it, and his *absolutely honest* deductions, comments, and views upon the different phases of life he passes through." It was not to be autobiography: "most autobiographies are insincere from beginning to end. About the only chance for the truth to be told is in fiction."

But this novel remains without a title in the list of unwritten books. Whether, if it had been written, it would have proved him as great an artist on the larger canvas as he is on the smaller, is a vain speculation and a matter of no moment. What matters is that in these twelve volumes of his he has done enough to add much and permanently to the world's sources of pleasure, and enough to give him an assured place among the masters of modern fiction.

THE MISADVENTURES IN MUSICAL COMEDY OF O. HENRY AND FRANKLIN P. ADAMS *

A CHICAGO manager started the trouble. He wrote as follows to Mr. Adams:

I am very anxious to secure a piece on the lines of "The Time, the Place, and the Girl." I say that for the reason that I have a star who is really a sensation, and we want to get him a piece that will suit him. It must be a modern character as he is a nice-looking fellow and I believe in a man continuing in a character in which he has achieved success. He is quite a fast talker, natty, dances very well, and sings excellently and is in every way very clever. We will have an opportunity to do a piece here by April and my ambition now is to get a play for him.

O. Henry has written a story for *Collier's* that fits Y—— to the ground. How would you like to coöperate with him?

The foregoing letter was received February 10, 1909. Mr. Adams welcomed the opportunity it presented, and took kindly to the idea of collaborating with O. Henry.

* Adapted from "Lo, the Poor Musical Comedy," by Franklin P. Adams, published in *The Success Magazine,* October, 1910.

He says: "I called on O. Henry and we discussed it at length. His other pseudonym was Barkis. We agreed to collaborate, both of us to work on the dialogue and both on the lyrics. And as it happened it was almost a complete collaboration. Hardly an independent line was written. . . .

"We were interested in the piece and anxious to please the manager who had gone out of his way to get us. . . . O. Henry and I would convene nearly every afternoon and talk the thing over, outlining scenes, making notes of lines of dialogue, tentative ideas for lyrics, etc. . . . We enjoyed working at this time. It was fun blocking out the plans and O. Henry was simply shedding whimsical ideas for lines and situations."

The plot concerned an anthropological expedition to Yucatan to inquire into the theory that the American Indian was descended from the ancient Aztecs. O. Henry called this *aztechnology* and "The Enthusiaztecs" was at first suggested for the title; but the manager would have none of it—was pleased to say that it sounded like the title of an amateur performance given by the Lincoln Memorial High School, and even went so far as to accuse the librettists of offences smacking not a little of the crime of highbrowism.

However, "The title inspiration soon came," says Mr. Adams. "It was O. Henry's and I am still of the opinion that it was an excellent title—'Lo.' As originally written the comedy emphasized the reversion

Misadventures in Musical Comedy

to type of the Indian, and tried to show, as Pope suggested, after

> 'Lo, the poor Indian! whose untutored mind
> Sees God in clouds, or hears him in the wind. . . .'

that

> 'To be, contents his natural desire.
> He asks no angel's wing, no seraph's fire.'"

The manager accepted this title with enthusiasm, for "You can advertise it easy and it looks good in type."

They had supposed that in the construction of a musical comedy the librettist first wrote some verses and the composer then evolved a melody to fit them. "But," Mr. Adams states, "most of our songs were constructed to fit tunes the composer had already written. I am not saying that this method is absolutely wrong, but it is infinitely harder work for the lyricist. Take an unfamiliar melody—often irregular as to meter—and try to fit intelligible, singable, rhythmical words to it. No wonder that after a month or two of it the barber tells you that it's getting pretty thin on top."

Difficulties and disagreements with the manager now came thick and fast: " 'Two and two,' says the manager, profoundly and confidentially, 'are five.' 'But'—you begin. 'You're inexperienced,' says the manager, 'and you don't know; *believe me*. I've been in this business twenty-seven years. We need comedy here. Laughs is what we want, all the time.' "

The infallible manager became convinced of the hopelessness of their ignorance of practical theatrical exigencies. "The second act was bad, the first scene was an interior," etc., etc. He engaged another man to rewrite the book. This was done. The manager approved the new man's outline. But his dialogue was rejected wholly, and the original collaborators had more rewriting to do. O. Henry never worked harder or more conscientiously on anything in his life. He lost weight. He worried. Day and night they worked on the comedy. Again they sent on the completed script, this being the third or fourth "rewrite." As they mailed it, O. Henry recited in a singular minor key:

> "Dramatization is vexation;
> Revision is as bad;
> This comedy perplexes me
> And managers drive me mad!"

Followed more dissatisfaction on the manager's part, and several harassing trips to Chicago.

But, finally, "Lo" was produced. Mr. Adams tells the tale: "The first performance was given in Aurora, Illinois, on August 25, 1909. With two exceptions—any members of the company who chance to read this will wonder who the second one I have in mind is—the acting was mediocre. But it 'went' well and the unbiased Auroran seemed to like it. I rather enjoyed it myself. There was no Night of Triumph, however. After the performance the manager met me on the street. 'Come to my room before you go to bed,' he said. 'Got to fix up that second act. It's rotten. . . .' So I did some more rewriting, which I think was never even tried out. I never heard of it, at any rate.

"After performances in Waukegan, Illinois, and Janesville, Wisconsin, 'Lo' opened in Milwaukee for a week's engagement. It seemed to please; the newspapers 'treated us lovely,' as the management had it.

"But at the age of fourteen weeks it breathed its last, on December 5th, in St. Joseph, Missouri. Its parents, bearing up nobly, learned the sad news through a stray newspaper paragraph. . . .

"That is the plain, unjapalacked story. I'm not recriminating. Taking one consideration with another, however, the librettist's lot is not a snappy one."

What Mr. Adams calls "Lo, the Poor Musical Comedy," is dead and gone, and no man knoweth the place of its sepulture. But most of the lyrics have survived.

Mr. Adams tells us that his collaboration with O. Henry was unusually thoroughgoing—hardly an independent line was written. But "Snap Shots" was all O. Henry's.

SNAP SHOTS

Watch out, lovers, when you promenade;
When you kiss and coo, in the deep moon shade.
When you're close together in the grape-vine swing,
When you are a-courting or philandering.
Mabel, Maud and Ann, Nellie, May and Fan,
Keep your eyes open for the Snap Shot Man!

Snap! Shots! Hear the shutter close!
What a world of roguishness the little snapper shows!
Click! Click! Caught you unaware—
Snap Shot Man'll get you if you don't take care!

Watch out, you, Sir, when your wife's away,
When you take your "cousin" to see the play,
With best aisle seats and in the bass drum row,
And holding her hand when all the lights are low.
Billy, Bob and Dan, Smith and Harrigan,
Keep your eyes open for the Snap Shot Man!

Snap! Shot! Hear the snapper snap!
Got you just as safe as any squirrel in a trap.
Click! Click! Got you just as slick—
Cam'ra man'll snap you if you don't be quick!

When you're swimming in your bathing suit,
And Hubby's in town, slaving like a brute,
And handsome young stranger, "Teach you how to swim?"
It's not my affair, it's up to you and him.
But, Adele and Pearl, in the water's swirl,
Keep your eyes open for the Snap Shot Girl.

Snap! Shots! Just a button pressed—
Only seems a trifle, but the courts'll do the rest.
Click! Click! Caught you P. Q. D.
Snap Shot Girl'll get you if you trifle in the sea.

"In Yucatan," of course owes its inspiration to O. Henry's sojourn in the exiles' haven, Honduras. But its lyrical tone is so strong, the farcical so nearly absent, that one guesses it to be mainly from the pen of Mr. Adams.

IN YUCATAN

In a *dolce far niente*
Mood amid the fruits and flowers,
Ladies in a land of plenty
Idly watch the ebbing hours;
In this paradise Utopian
Time and tide are cornucopian;
So we say *"Festina lente,"*
All the sands of time are ours.

In Yucatan, in Yucatan,
Land of eternal lotus chewing,
In Yucatan, in Yucatan,
Where sunny skies are blue as bluing,
In Yucatan, in Yucatan,
Oh, land of honeyed "Nothing Doing,"
Land of lyric, love, and leisure,
Place of poetry and pleasure,
Fairy-land of "Nothing Doing"—
Yucatan—in Yucatan.

Banish we the thoughts of sorrow
In this country of the blest;
Brood we not on a to-morrow,
Life is only brief at best.
In this land of summer season,
Reck we not of rhyme or reason,
As we puff the mild cigarro,
Singing "Life's a merry jest."

In Yucatan, in Yucatan,
Land of eternal lotus chewing,
In Yucatan, in Yucatan,
Where sunny skies are blue as bluing,
In Yucatan, in Yucatan,
Oh, land of honeyed "Nothing Doing,"

Land of lyric, love, and leisure,
Place of poetry and pleasure,
Fairy-land of "Nothing Doing"—
Yucatan—in Yucatan.

The following group of five songs was probably written soon after the collaborators had received a managerial lecture on the practical requirements of the theatre. They breathe the spirit of stagy sophistication as to "what they want," and "how to get it over."

LET US SING

There is nothing new, my lady, in the lexicon of love;
It is all as old as time.
They were vowing by the moon and to the twinkling stars above,
When they handed Eve the lime.
There is nothing new to tell you, there is nothing to sing,
There is nothing new to say;
So you'll have to be contented with the ordinary thing,
In the ordinary way.

Let us sing in the manner traditional,
For we must have a lovers' duet,
With a silly refrain repetitional
In a chorus you cannot forget.
They'll applaud from Topeka to Gloversville,
At the mention of "Love" or a "Kiss";
Oh, you bet we are lovers from Loversville
And we love in a lyric like this:—

LOVE IS ALL THAT MATTERS

An audience is generally clamorous,
For something in the nature of a waltz;
Be it ne'er so senseless.

Wherefore-less and whence-less,
Be its logic ne'er so full of faults,
Just let the theme and melody be amorous,
And let the honeyed sentiment be plain;
If the music's tuneful,
If the words are spoon-ful,
Love is all you need in a refrain.

> For love is all that matters
> In a waltz refrain—
> A lilt that softly patters
> Like a summer rain;
> A theme that's worn to tatters;
> And an ancient strain.
> Yet love is all that matters
> In a waltz refrain.

Now I might sing a song of high society,
And I might sing about a lot of things;
I might spend the time on
Warbling you a rhyme on
Anything from cabbages to kings.
But though I have an infinite variety
Of themes that I might sing about to you,
There is only one thing,
Though an overdone thing,
Love, the olden theme that's always new.

> For love is all that matters
> In a waltz refrain—
> A lilt that softly patters
> Like a summer rain;
> A theme that's worn to tatters;
> And an ancient strain.
> Yet love is all that matters
> In a waltz refrain.

Let who will construct a nation's laws if I may write its
 songs,
As the poet used to say;
Though it's absolutely simple if you figure what belongs
To the usual National lay.
Take the songs of Andalusia as presented on the stage
By a dashing young brunette,
Who can stamp her feet in anger and can snap her eyes in
 rage,
And can smoke a cigarette.

> Let us sing in a manner Castilian
> To the twang of the gladsome guitar,
> With a colour scheme black and vermilion,
> And the music staccato bizarre;
> Let us sing all that sad señorita stuff
> To a dance that is mildly insane;
> Let us steal all that old Carmencita stuff,
> That's the way of the lovers in Spain:—

CARAMBA

Spanish Burlesque Song

> Caramba di Sar-sa-pa-ril-li-o,
> Cinchona, Peruna, Mon-doo;
> Bologna, Cologna, Vanillio,
> Northwestern and eke "C.B.Q."
> Oh, Chilli con carne and Piccolo—
> Mazeppa di Buffalo Bill—
> So hurry and drop in your nickel-o,
> Caramba di Sar-sa-pa-rill!

Backward, turn a little backward, Father Tempus in thy
 flight,
To the days of long ago;
When Variety was funny and a "team" was a delight
In a biff-bang slap-stick show.

If you'll give us your attention for a moment we will try
Quite a job of comedy,
For a couple of comedians you see in she and I,
As you can quite plainly see.

    Let us sing in a way vaudevillian,
    In the way of the "ten-twenty-thirt"
    When the "Varnishes" (Eddie and Lillian)
    Made you laugh till you honestly hurt.
    Let us hand out a sad little "mother" song,
    In a way that is truly refined;
    Let us follow it up with another song,
    Of the best song-and-danciest kind:—

NEVER FORGET YOUR PARENTS

    A young man once was sitting
    Within a swell café,
    The music it did play so sweet,
    The people were so gay.
    But he alone was silent,
    A tear was in his eye,
    A waitress she stepped up to him,
    And asked him gently why.
    He turned to her in sorrow,
    And at first he spoke no word;
    But soon he spoke unto her,
    For she was an honest girl.
    He rose up from that table,
    In that elegant café,
    And in a voice replete with tears,
    To her, he then did say:

    "Never forget your father
    Think all he done for you
    Do not desert your mother dear,
    So loving, kind, and true
    Think of all they have gave you—

>   Do not cast it away—
>   For if it had not been for them
>   We would not be here to-day."

WHILE STROLLING THRO' THE FOREST

>   While strolling thro' the forest
>   Upon a summer's day,
>   I chanced to see, and she smiled at me,
>   A lady and her name was May.
>   Oh my! Wasn't she a beaut!
>   Root-ti-toot, ti-toot-ti-toot-ti-toot!
>   She's the neatest, she's the sweetest,
>   She's also the completest.
>   She's the lady who I dearly love,
>   And—ah—this is—ah—what she said:
>
>   We have tried for to amuse you
>   With our remarks so bright,
>   And now that we have finished,
>   We're going to say good-night.
>   We are chatty, we are happy,
>   And we think the same of you,
>   And with your kind permission
>   We're going to say "Adoo."

"Dear Yankee Maid," one guesses, was intended to suit the requirements of the manager's protégé, the nice-looking fellow who danced well and sang excellently; and "You May Always Be My Sweetheart" was a duet to be sung probably by this paragon and the leading lady.

DEAR YANKEE MAID

>   There's a lilt that is tuneful and fetchin'!
>   When you sing of an Irish colleen;
>   And the lyrical praise of a Gretchen

Is a theme that is fit for a queen;
The bewitching young lady of Paris—
She may hold many fast in her thrall—
But this song (which is published by Harris)
Is to tell of the best of them all.

    O Yankee maid! My Yankee maid!
    You are the one best bet.
    You are the goods, with duty prepaid.
    You are the finest yet.
    I am for you, brown eyes or blue,
    Tresses of gold or jet.
    I serenade you, Yankee maid;
    You are the one best bet.

Of the maiden seductive and Spanish,
There is many a song has been sung.
And the ladies Norwegian and Danish
Were a theme when Columbus was young;
Oh, the ladies of England are pretty;
There are those who declare for the Jap.
But the best is the girl of this ditty,
Yankee maids are the best on the map.

    O Yankee maid! My Yankee maid!
    You are the one best bet.
    You are the goods, with duty prepaid.
    You are the finest yet.
    I am for you, brown eyes or blue,
    Tresses of gold or jet.
    I serenade you, Yankee maid;
    You are the one best bet.

YOU MAY ALWAYS BE MY SWEETHEART
(If You Care to Be)

A maid of simple station, I, unlearned in lovers' lore,
    Sweetly shy;
The art of osculation I had never tried before,
    Which is why
Your recent demonstration of that proud and manly art—
    Is it plain?—
Has caused a queer sensation in the region of my heart,
    And this refrain:

    I've never had a sweetheart, for I've been fancy free.
    My heart's been locked to lovers, and there's no key.
    But if you should continue to be so kind to me,
    You may always be my sweetheart if you care to be.

Dear Madam: Contents noted in your favour of this date;
    I remain
As ever, Yours Devotedly—P. S., I beg to state
    And explain
Your recent proposition has a sweet and pleasant sound
    To my ears,
'Twill be my fond ambition just to have you stick around
    A million years.
I've never had a sweetheart, for I've been fancy free.
My heart's been locked to lovers, and there's no key.
But if you should continue to be so kind to me,
I will always be your sweetheart if you'll let me be.

The "Statue Song" was written as a substitute for one the composer was guilty of, to fit a tune which was described as "a lutherburbank of 'Anitra's Dance' in the Peer Gynt suite and Moskowski's 'Spanish Dance.'"

STATUE SONG

Idol of my race I sing,
Humbly kneeling at thy shrine.
Take the sacrifice I bring;
All that I possess is thine:

Humbly kneeling at thy shrine,
Let me chant my idol song,
All that I possess is thine,
I have loved thee overlong,

Let me chant my idol song.
Take the sacrifice I bring.
I have loved thee overlong.
Idol of my race I sing.

Beloved let me lay these at thy feet—
These flowers of forgetfulness so sweet.
Forsake thou thoughts of other days and pride,
And come thou back with me, thine Indian bride,
Untamed and free.
Return to me
Thine own predestined bride.

"Little Old Main Street" is a protest and natural reaction from the wave of Broadway and Little-Old-New York songs which for so long inundated long-suffering Oshkosh and Kalamazoo.

LITTLE OLD MAIN STREET

Singers may boast about Broadway,
And they most gen'rally do:
Spring all that flowery fluff on the Bowery—
Take it. I'll stake it to you;

Call me a yap if you care to,
Say I'm a rube or a shine,
But give me the street that has got 'em all beat—
Little old Main Street for mine.

Little old Main Street for mine!
Take a look at the lovers in line—
Three village charmers and twenty-eight farmers,
All meeting the six-twenty-nine—
Little old Main Street for mine,
When you're back with the pigs and the kine,
Broadway and such for Your Uncle? Not much
For it's Little old Main Street for mine.

Sing if you must of your State Street,
Sing of the Bois and the Strand,
And if you have a new song of the Avenue,
Sing it to beat the old band!
Sing of the streets of the city,
Not for Yours Truly—"Uh, Uh!"
But give me the street of the village élite;
Little old Main Street for *muh!*

Little old Main Street for mine,
And right down by the Post Office sign
Hear 'em say "Well, what a long rainy spell!
But it looks like to-morrow'll be fine."
Little old Main Street for mine,
Where it's dead at a quarter past nine
See the folks flock past the Opry-House block,
Oh, it's little old Main Street for mine.

"It's the Little Things that Count," even in the success of a musical comedy. A few trifles like the following would have gone far toward making a Broadway success.

IT'S THE LITTLE THINGS THAT COUNT

Girl— Little drops of water, little grains of sand,
　　　Make the mighty ocean and the pleasant land
Boy— Little drops of seltzer, little drops of rye,
　　　Make the pleasant highball, when a man is dry.
Both—It's the little things that count, ev'rywhere you go;
　　　Trifles make a large amount. Don't you find it so?
Girl— Little deeds of kindness, little words of love,
　　　Make our life an Eden, like the heaven above.
Boy— Little drops of promise, made to little wives,
　　　Make us little fibbers all our little lives.
Both—It's the little things that count, ev'rywhere you go;
　　　Trifles make a large amount. Don't you find it so?

O. HENRY IN HIS OWN BAGDAD

By George Jean Nathan

In the summer of 1908 William Sydney Porter and Robert Hobart Davis, alias "O. Henry" and "Bob" Davis respectively—and likewise respectively one of the greatest of American short-story writers and one of the greatest rejectors of all species of stories—were discussing the merits and demerits of New York City during the tropical, asphalt-smelly season. "Let's get out of it for a few days," suggested Davis. "I'll take you to a wonderful place down on Long Island, where the fishing is immense and the fish correspondingly large."

"Well," said Henry, "New York is a bit warm and I'll just take you up."

They started. They arrived. Fishing tackle was put in order; collars and coats were cast aside; Henry expressed admiration at the ability of the masculine natives to expectorate tobacco juice "as far as the eye could see"; Davis lit a cigar; and the expedition was off. It was a mile walk. "We won't ride, because the exercise will do us good," suggested Davis. Henry assented. The day was gray-blue and sizzling. They had not gone more than three city blocks when Henry was already drenched with perspiration. But he kept on manfully. A little way farther on, however, Davis noticed that his companion was desperately endeavouring to find something in his trousers' pockets. "What are you looking for?" he asked. "I am looking for my return ticket to New York," replied Henry, positively, "and let me tell you that as soon as I find it, I'm going to take a 'hitch' on a wagon and go back—fast! I know it's blamed hot in town, but there are just as good fish left on the menu as there are in the sea."

"Bagdad," as O. Henry referred to New York in his modern Arabian Nights, was, in his own words to a close friend, "the cosy haven for everybody, including amateur fishermen and other disappointed persons." O. Henry loved the metropolis, and its intense heat or cold made little change in his affection for it. "If you like the city so well, then," he was once asked, "why do you live in Asheville so much of the time?" "Because," he answered, "New York gets into my veins so strongly that I have to go away from it when I want to work. For the same reason, I venture, that a man who is deeply in love with a woman can't think of anything but that woman when he is anywhere near her."

During his frequent visits in his own skyscraper-filled Bagdad, this literary Haroun-al-Raschid prowled about in curious corners, brushed up against curious individuals, and ferreted out curious secrets, curious heart mysteries, and curious little lights on the human machine—all of which subsequently found their way into his stories. Some of his adventures while Haroun-al-Raschiding must, therefore, possess interest for the vast reading throng that has smiled and felt a tear while turning his pages. It was during one of his prowling tours several years ago that O. Henry, with H. H. McClure, who suggested the writing of the modern Arabian Nights tales to the short-story king, was seated in a Broadway restaurant at luncheon. "What are you going to do to-night?" asked McClure. "I'm going to persuade a 'hobo' to give me three hundred dollars," answered the writer. "On a bet?" asked McClure. "Not at all," replied O. Henry, "that's the price of a story and I'm going to rub up against some tramps down on the Bowery until one of them suggests the plot to me." That night O. Henry did travel downtown and started on a Haroun-al-Raschid expedition in the vicinity of the famous bread-line. His genial, well-fleshed personality always stood him in good stead, and no matter how tough the community he chanced to enter, unpleasantness of any sort was a rare occurrence. When he talked with a "hobo" he was a "hobo." When he talked with a railroad president he was a railroad president. O. Henry was a chameleon of conversation and of what is known colloquially as "front." He always took on the air—it seemed—of the person to whom he was talking. One of his friends has said of him that there was no better "mixer" in the world—and the truth of the statement is borne out by a survey of the intimate and varied insight revealed in his diverse writings.

On the night in question O. Henry moved around among the Bowery derelicts until he finally got into touch with a typical "bum." They strolled down the street a way together and asked a passer-by for the time. "Almost midnight," said the latter. "Gee," remarked Henry to his tattered companion. "I feel like a cup o' coffee. Come on, I've got a quarter and we'll blow some of it in this place." They entered the dingy eating-house, sat up to the counter and each ordered a cup of coffee and a ham sandwich. Although the two men had now been together for some time, the short-story writer had detected the gleam of nothing definite in the tramp that promised to provide the "copy" he was seeking. But he felt sure he had picked his man right and he felt equally sure that the fellow sooner or later would unconsciously suggest to him something or other by which he would profit. O. Henry rarely "led" the conversation. He preferred to let it come naturally. He said nothing to his companion, who was busily concerning himself with the food before him. When they had finished and had reached the street, Henry suggested that they walk leisurely up the Bowery and see if there was anything to be seen. They wandered around aimlessly for fully an hour and a half and then Henry said he felt like having another cup of coffee. The two men went into another eating-place and ordered two cups of coffee—at two cents a cup. Then they walked around some more, but still Henry had succeeded in getting no idea from his bedraggled companion. Finally, tired out, he told the latter he was going to leave him. He reached out his hand to "shake" with the tramp and, as their hands met, Henry suddenly surprised the "hobo" by laughing. "What's up, cull?" asked the latter. "Oh, nothin'," replied Henry, "I just thought of something." This was true, as he afterward confessed, the "something" in point having been an odd twist for a new story. But the oddest twist to this particular Haroun-al-Raschid anecdote—and a typical O. Henry twist it is—is the fact that the idea O. Henry suddenly got for his story had absolutely nothing to do with the Bowery, with tramps, with two-cent coffee, or anything even remotely related thereto. "Well, then," remarked a friend to whom he had narrated the incident, "what good did the Bowery sojourn do you? You didn't get your three-hundred-dollar idea from a tramp after all, did you?"

"Indeed, I did," replied O. Henry. "That is, in a way. The tramp didn't give me the idea, to be sure, but he did not drive it out of my head—which is just as important. If I had not gone down on the Bowery and had chosen an uptown friend for a companion instead of that tramp, my more cultured companion would not have allowed me a moment's conversational respite in which my mind could have worked, and, as a consequence, the idea would never have come to me. So, you see, the Bowery 'hobo' served a lot of good, after all."

Strolling through Madison Square one night after the theatre, O. Henry came upon a young girl crying

as if her heart were surely cracking, if not already
broken. The man with Henry, his pity and sympathy
aroused, walked over to the girl, touched her on the
shoulder, and inquired into the cause of her grief. It
developed that the girl had come to the city from a
town in central New Jersey, had lost her way, and was
without money, friends, or a place to sleep. Deeply
touched, the man with the short-story writer gave the
girl a couple of dollars, put her in charge of a policeman, whose latent sympathy he managed to arouse with
a one-dollar bill, and, satisfied with his act of charity,
locked arms with Henry and continued on through the
dark square toward Twenty-third Street. "Why
didn't you speak to her?" he asked Henry. "I'll bet
there was a corking story in that girl that you could
have dragged out." O. Henry smiled. "Old man," he
said, "there never is a story where there seems to be one.
That's one rule I always work on—it saves time and,
let me see—two plus one—yes, three dollars!"

O. Henry's metropolitan sales- and shop-girl types
are well known to his readers. "Do you ever go into
the department stores to study them?" some one once
asked the writer. "Indeed, not," answered the latter.
"It is not the sales-girl in the department store who is
worth studying, it is the sales-girl out of it. You can't
get romance over a counter."

With two friends O. Henry was walking down Broadway one evening in December—Broadway, the sack of
New York "life," the big paper Bagdad out of which

O. Henry drew many of his characters. Near Herald Square the men were approached by a rather well-dressed young man who, in a calm, gentle voice, told his "hard luck story" and begged for the "loan" of a quarter. One of the men handed over the twenty-five cents to the stranger and the latter disappeared quickly 'round the corner into Thirty-sixth Street. "Seemed like an honest, worthy chap," remarked the man who had parted with the quarter. "Yes," added O. Henry quietly, "he seemed like an honest, worthy chap to me, too—last night."

While walking down Broadway on another occasion, O. Henry accidentally bumped against a man who was not looking in the direction he was walking. "I beg your pardon," said Henry, "but really you ought to look where you are going." "If I did in this town, I probably wouldn't go," replied the man with a sarcastic smile. "Ah," said O. Henry, quickly, "and how are all the folks in Chicago?"

When O. Henry collaborated with F. P. Adams in writing the libretto for the musical comedy "Lo," a friend said to him: "Adams says he got the idea for his share of the play from a cheque for advance royalties. Where did you get the idea for your share?" "From the *hope* for a cheque for advance royalties," he answered.

While "Harouning" along the river front one night, O. Henry happened upon a couple of sailors, one of whom was much the worse for liquor. "I see your friend is intoxicated," he remarked to the sober sailor. "You don't say!" exclaimed the latter in mock astonishment. And the short-story king appreciated the answer at his expense as much as did those to whom he subsequently repeated it. O. Henry never missed a favourable opportunity to have a chat with an amiable policeman. "Policemen know so many odd things and so few necessary ones," he would remark. While talking with one of the blue-coats in Hell's Kitchen one night, years ago, Henry said that they were suddenly startled—at least, that he was—by two loud revolver shots. "Some one's been killed!" he exclaimed. "No, don't worry," returned the "cop," coolly, "only injured. It takes at least three bullets to kill any one in this part of town."

O. HENRY—APOTHECARY *

By Christopher Morley

Where once he used camphor, glycerin,
   Cloves, aloes, potash, peppermint in bars,
And all the oils and essences so keen
   That druggists keep in rows of stoppered jars—
Now, blender of strange drugs more volatile,
   The master pharmacist of joy and pain
Dispenses sadness tinctured with a smile
   And laughter that dissolves in tears again.

O brave apothecary! You who knew
   What dark and acid doses life prefers,
And yet with smiling face resolved to brew
   These sparkling potions for your customers—
Glowing with globes of red and purple glass
   Your window gladdens travellers who pass.

* From a volume of Mr. Morley's poems published by the George H. Doran Company.

O. HENRY*

By William Lyon Phelps

IN North Carolina they have just erected a memorial to "O. Henry." He was a profoundly sincere artist, as is shown, not only in his finished work but in his private correspondence. His worst defect was a fear and hatred of conventionality; he had such mortal terror of stock phrases that, as some one has said, he wrote no English at all—he wrote the dot, dash, telegraphic style. Yet leaving aside all his perversities and his whimsicalities, and the poorer part of his work where the desire to be original is more manifest than any valuable result of it, there remain a sufficient number of transcripts from life and interpretations of it to give him abiding fame. There is a humorous tenderness in The Whirligig of Life,† and profound ethical passion in A Blackjack Bargainer.† A highly intelligent though unfavourable criticism of Porter that came to me in a private letter—I wish it might be printed—condemns him for the vagaries of his plots —which remind my correspondent of the quite serious

* From "The Advance of the English Novel," by William Lyon Phelps; Dodd, Mead & Co., 1916.
† See "Whirligigs."

criticism he read in a Philadelphia newspaper, which spoke of "the interesting but hardly credible adventures of Ulysses." Now hyperbole is a great American failing; and Porter was so out and out American that this disease of art raised blotches on his work. Yet his best emphasis is placed where it belongs.

No writer of distinction has, I think, been more closely identified with the short story in English than O. Henry. Irving, Poe, Hawthorne, Bret Harte, Stevenson, Kipling attained fame in other fields; but although Porter had his mind fully made up to launch what he hoped would be the great American novel, the veto of death intervened, and the many volumes of his "complete works" are made up of brevities. The essential truthfulness of his art is what gave his work immediate recognition, and accounts for his rise from journalism to literature. There is poignancy in his pathos; desolation in his tragedy; and his extraordinary humour is full of those sudden surprises that give us delight. Uncritical readers have never been so deeply impressed with O. Henry as have the professional jaded critics, weary of the old trick a thousand times repeated, who found in his writings a freshness and originality amounting to genius.

ABOUT NEW YORK WITH O. HENRY
By Arthur Bartlett Maurice

I

THE HEART OF O'HENRY-LAND

IRVING PLACE, beginning at Fourteenth Street, runs north for six blocks to perish against the iron palings that line the southerly side of Gramercy Park. Half way up, on the west side of the thoroughfare, between Seventeenth and Eighteenth streets, there is a dingy, four-story, brownstone house. The shutters are up. The casements of the upper stories frame vacancy. That vacancy stares down at the passer-by with a kind of hurt blindness. It is as if the structure itself was conscious of an imminent demise, of a swiftly coming demolition. For next year, next month, next week, to-morrow, perhaps, the old ramshackle edifice will be gone, with a towering skyscraper springing up on the site. The number of the building is 55. There, in the front room on the second floor, William Sydney Porter lived in the days when he was learning to read the heart of the Big City of Razzle-Dazzle. And as he was constitutionally opposed to anything that involved arduous physical exercise, the quintessence of O'Henry-Land lies within a circle of half a mile radius, with No. 55 as the centre.

Within that circle may be found the hotels of the Spanish-American New York stories, Chubbs' Third Avenue Restaurant, the Old Munich of The Halberdier of the Little Rheinschloss,* the particular saloon which served as the background for The Lost Blend †—as a matter of fact that saloon is directly across the street from No. 55 and behind the bar there presides a white-aproned, genial cocktail mixer who will answer to the name of "Con" just as in the story —the four sides of Gramercy Park which are so conspicuous in the tales of aristocratic flavour, the bench —which could be confused with no other bench in the world—which Stuffy Pete, one of Two Thanksgiving-day Gentlemen,† regarded in the light of personal property, and those other benches in the other square, a few blocks to the north, where prepossessing young women, inspired by Robert Louis Stevenson's "New Arabian Nights," were moved to romantic narrative, where disconsolate caliphs, shorn of their power, sat brooding over the judgments of Allah, where fifth wheels rolled along asphalted pavements and djinns came obedient to the rubbing of the lamp.

To Mr. Robert Rudd Whiting, with whom he had been associated in the early days when he first began

* See "Roads of Destiny."
† See "The Trimmed Lamp."

About New York With O. Henry

to contribute to the columns of *Ainslee's Magazine*, Sydney Porter once extended a luncheon invitation. It was to be a Spanish-American luncheon in the course of which O. Henry was to introduce his guest to certain flavours and dishes that he himself had learned to like or at least to endure in the days of his exile in the Lands of the Lotus Eaters. The two men were crossing Union Square. "Come with me," said Porter, "I will show you the real place. Over at M——'s [he mentioned a restaurant in a street to the south] you may find the Señors, the Capitans, the Majors, the Colonels. But if you would sit with the Generalissimos, the Imperators, the truly exalted who hail from Central and South American countries, accept my guiding hand." So from the Square they turned in Fifteenth Street and found, on the south side, some seventy-five yards east of Fourth Avenue, the Hotel America, with its clientele of gesticulating Latins, who, if not planning revolution, had all the outward appearance of arch-conspirators. It was the atmosphere that went to the making of The Gold that Glittered,* which, if the reader remembers, began at the very spot at which the invitation had been extended "where Broadway skirts the corner of the Square presided over by George the Veracious."

The Halberdier of the Little Rheinschloss † dealt with a restaurant which O. Henry designated as Old

* See "Strictly Business."
† See "Roads of Destiny."

Munich. Long ago, the story-teller told us, it was the resort of interesting Bohemians, but now "only artists and musicians and literary folk frequent it." For many years, so the tale runs, the customers of Old Munich have accepted the place as a faithful copy from the ancient German town. The big hall, with its smoky rafters, rows of imported steins, portrait of Goethe, and verses printed on the walls—translated into German from the original of the Cincinnati Poets—seemed atmospherically correct when viewed through the bottom of a glass. Then the proprietors rented the room above, called it the Little Rheinschloss, and built in a stairway. Up there was an imitation stone parapet, ivy-covered, and the walls painted to represent depth and distance, with the Rhine winding at the base of the vineyarded slopes and the Castle of Ehrenbreitstein looming directly opposite the entrance. To Old Munich came the young man with the wrecked good clothes and the hungry look, to assume the armour of the ancient halberdier and, on a certain momentous evening, to be confiscated by the aristocrats to serve menially at the banquet-board.

As the tale had always been an especial favourite, the present writer had ventured into many parts of the city in his search for the background that would best fit the O. Henry description. For a time the hunt seemed vain. But one day he spoke to Mr. Gilman Hall on the subject. The latter laughed. "Do I know the real Old Munich? Very well, indeed. Often I dined there with Porter. No wonder you have not found it. You have been looking too far to the north, to the south, to the west. Don't you realize that Porter would never have walked that far if he could have helped it? The only time I ever persuaded him afoot as far as Seventy-second Street and Riverside Drive, he stopped, and, with an injured air, asked if we had not yet passed Peekskill. We are just before his old home, No. 55. Why not try round the corner?" So fifty feet to the south, and a short block to the east, in the restaurant and beer-hall known to some as Allaire's and to others as Scheffel Hall, the setting of the tale was found. There was a natural free-hand swing to certain parts of the O. Henry descriptions, but even without the corroboration of those who knew personally of Porter's associations with the place, one glance at the long raftered room is enough to stamp it as the place where the waiter known simply as No. 18 witnessed the comedy of the hot soup tureen and the blistered hands, and William Deering finished the three months of earning his own living without once being discharged for incompetence.

II

THE O. HENRY APPEAL

Three or four years ago, in the columns of a literary magazine of which he was then the editor, the present writer invited the expression of various opinions with the idea of finding out which of the stories of O. Henry had had the widest appeal. To the person whom he then designated as The Thousandth Reader he presented ten volumes of the short stories. She was being introduced for the first time to the work of O. Henry, and for a month, day after day, she gave herself over to the two hundred and fifty odd tales of the modern Scheherazade. When she had finished the last story he asked her to jot down the names of the ten that had most appealed to her, in the order of their appeal. Her choice was in many ways so surprising that it suggested the symposium. This was the list of The Thousandth Reader:

1. A Municipal Report.
2. The Pendulum.
3. A Blackjack Bargainer.
4. A Retrieved Reformation.
5. The Furnished Room.
6. The Hypotheses of Failure.
7. Roads of Destiny.
8. Next to Reading Matter.
9. The Enchanted Profile.
10. Two Renegades.

To that list the present writer decided to add nine others. First were three from men who were themselves spinners of tales, Booth Tarkington, Owen Johnson, and George Barr McCutcheon.

Mr. Tarkington, commenting upon his list, said: "The ten are not his best stories. I don't know which his 'best' are, of course. These ten are what

About New York With O. Henry 113

you asked for—the ten I have enjoyed most. There is one I wanted to include. The boy who went to war after the girl flouted him and came back the town hero and said to her (she was married then): 'Oh, I don't know—maybe I could if I tried!' but I couldn't remember the title and couldn't find it." (The title of the story Mr. Tarkington had in mind was The Moment of Victory in "Options.")

Mr. Tarkington's list:

1. The Ransom of Red Chief.
2. The Harbinger.
3. The Passing of Black Eagle.
4. Squaring the Circle.
5. Past One at Rooney's.
6. The Handbook of Hymen.
7. Strictly Business.
8. The Clarion Call.
9. Jeff Peters as a Personal Magnet.
10. The Memento.

The following titles represented the choice of Mr. Owen Johnson:

1. An Unfinished Story.
2. A Municipal Report.
3. The Rose of Dixie.
4. A Lickpenny Lover.
5. According to Their Lights.
6. Mammon and the Archer.
7. The Defeat of the City.
8. The Girl and the Graft.
9. The Shamrock and the Palm.
10. The Pendulum.

Mr. George Barr McCutcheon's list:

1. The Tale of a Tainted Tenner.
2. Let Me Feel Your Pulse.
3. A Fog in Santone.
4. The Lost Blend.
5. The Duplicity of Hargraves.
6. The Marquis and Miss Sally.
7. The Gift of the Magi.
8. A Cosmopolite in a Café.
9. According to Their Lights.
10. The Making of a New Yorker.

Fifth in order, but naturally first in sentimental interest, was the list indicating the feelings of The One Who Knew Him Best—Mrs. William Sydney Porter. It was in a very beautiful letter that Mrs. Porter told of her preferences. To her the stories *were* Mr. Porter. She found it hard to name them in a list in order. But immediately one story came to her mind. That was A Municipal Report.*

"After all," she wrote, "I am not sure that it is the story—good as it is—for O. Henry's own face lifts from a Nashville 'roast' that was given that story and I hear his puzzled, 'Why did it offend? Do you see anything in it that should offend?' The Fifth Wheel *—and we stand together on Madison Square in the deep snow, or the biting wind, looking at the line waiting for beds. When we turn away ten men have found shelter. The recording angel must have seen us there

* See "Strictly Business."

some of the snowy nights of 1908. He must have known that when we turned homeward there were times when O. Henry had not a dollar fifty left in his pocket." One story in Mrs. Porter's list likely to surprise readers is Madame Bo-Peep of the Ranches.* But Mrs. Porter said that that story figured largely in her own life. In the spring of 1905 her mother came home from Greensboro and said to her: "Your old friend Will Porter is a writer. He lives in New York and writes under the name of O. Henry." "O. Henry! In my desk lay Madame Bo-Peep and I loved her. I wrote O. Henry a note. 'If you are not Will Porter don't bother to answer,' I said. He bothered to answer. The letter came as fast as Uncle Sam could bring it. 'Some day when you are not real busy,' he wrote, 'won't you sit down at your desk where you keep those antiquated stories and write to me? I'd be so pleased to hear something about what the years have done for you, and what you think about when the tree frogs begin to holler in the evening.' Thus after many years a boy and girl friendship was renewed. Last in my list, but first in my heart, is Adventures in Neurasthenia, the new title, Let Me Feel Your Pulse,† the publishers gave. It brings back the little office in Asheville, the pad, empty except for the title and the words: 'So I went to a doctor.' So often at the last the pad was empty. The sharp pencil points in their waiting

* See "Whirligigs."
† See "Sixes and Sevens."

seemed to me to mock the empty pencil, the weary brain. The picture is too vivid." This was Mrs. Porter's list:

1. A Municipal Report.
2. The Fifth Wheel.
3. A Lickpenny Lover.
4. A Doubledyed Deceiver.
5. Brickdust Row.
6. The Trimmed Lamp.
7. The Brief Début of 'Tildy.
8. An Unfinished Story.
9. Madame Bo-Peep of the Ranches.
10. Let Me Feel Your Pulse.

The sixth list was from a man (incidentally he was one of O. Henry's closest friends in the New York years) who has read, accepted, and rejected more short stories than any other man in the world. That man was Mr. Robert H. Davis, and among the accepted stories were many of the stories of O. Henry. Prefacing his selection, Mr. Davis expressed the opinion that The Last Leaf * would become more impressive as he grew older, whereas at the time of writing A Tempered Wind † and An Unfinished Story ‡ entertained him greatly. There were times when he laughed inordinately at The Handbook of Hymen § and Hostages to Momus.** "It is rather remarkable," wrote Mr.

* See "The Trimmed Lamp."
† See "The Gentle Grafter."
‡ See "The Four Million."
§ See "Heart of the West."
** See "The Gentle Grafter."

Davis, "that a man of his temperament could do so many good stories under the high pressure of necessity. He was buoyant and lazy in prosperity, depressed and productive in adversity. How few of the millions who read him know what it cost O. Henry to make them laugh!" These were the ten tales that had been caught in the meshes of Mr. Davis's memory:

1. A Tempered Wind.
2. The Last Leaf.
3. An Unfinished Story.
4. Hostages to Momus.
5. The Trimmed Lamp.
6. Friend Telemachus.
7. The Handbook of Hymen.
8. The Moment of Victory.
9. The Ethics of Pig.
10. A Technical Error.

The following list made by Mr. Arthur W. Page represents, in a measure, the opinion of Mr. Porter's publishers:

1. The Rose of Dixie.
2. The Gift of the Magi.
3. The Cop and the Anthem.
4. Let Me Feel Your Pulse.
5. An Unfinished Story.
6. A Municipal Report.
7. The Guardian of the Accolade.
8. Witches' Loaves.
9. Hearts and Crosses.
10. The Fifth Wheel.

Many persons have come forward claiming to have discovered O. Henry. Some of these claims have come from sources that would have moved Sydney Porter himself to mingled delight and astonishment. But the man who was responsible for O. Henry's going to New York, who persuaded the publisher of a magazine to forward the money that made the journey possible, was Mr. Gilman Hall. So among all claimants Mr. Hall has the best title to recognition as O. Henry's discoverer. Mr. Hall's list:

1. An Unfinished Story.
2. A Municipal Report.
3. Roads of Destiny.
4. The Buyer from Cactus City.
5. The Furnished Room.
6. The Passing of Black Eagle.
7. The Gift of the Magi.
8. From the Cabby's Seat.
9. Brickdust Row.
10. A Retrieved Reformation.

To the opinions of writers of stories and buyers of stories it was thought wise to add the point of view of those whose business it is to sell stories. Three literary agents were consulted. This is a composite list representing their opinions:

1. A Harlem Tragedy.
2. Mammon and the Archer.
3. A Lickpenny Lover.
4. The Furnished Room.
5. The Marry Month of May.
6. The Gift of the Magi.
7. The Enchanted Profile.
8. An Unfinished Story.

About New York With O. Henry

9. The Last Leaf.
10. The Thing's the Play.

In conclusion the present writer insisted on presenting a list indicating his own favourites. It was as follows:

1. The Defeat of the City.
2. Mammon and the Archer.
3. The Furnished Room.
4. The Shamrock and the Palm.
5. The Halberdier of the Rheinschloss.
6. The Lost Blend.
7. A Lickpenny Lover.
8. A Municipal Report.
9. Two Renegades.
10. Thimble, Thimble.

Curious, indeed, is the story told by these lists. It illustrates strikingly the wide range of O. Henry's appeal. Ten lists of ten tales apiece, and sixty-two different titles, most of them appearing on but one list. A few favourites there are: A Municipal Report * (the narrative which probably shows its author at the highwater mark of his powers) with six mentions; An Unfinished Story † with seven mentions; A Lickpenny Lover,‡ The Gift of the Magi,† and The Furnished Room,† with four mentions; and Mammon and the Archer † and Let Me Feel Your Pulse § with three

* See "Strictly Business."
† See "The Four Million."
‡ See "The Voice of the City."
§ See "Sixes and Sevens."

mentions. On the basis of these lists the New York stories have had the greatest appeal. Some of the individual selections were significant. For example, Mr. Tarkington picked as his first choice The Ransom of Red Chief,* a tale to be found in no other list. Perhaps that was only the expression of the mood of a moment, the liking of a man who during the previous two or three years had invented Hedrick Madison and Penrod Schofield for a delightfully diabolical boy.

III

THE "EAST SIDE" OF O. HENRY

In his nightly wanderings through his City of Bagdad, the good Haroun-al-Raschid in his golden prime did not confine himself to those thoroughfares that were analogous to London's Park Lane, Paris's Avenue Bois de Boulogne, or New York's Riverside Drive. On the contrary, he preferred to seek out the purlieus, and to listen wisely in the humble shop of "Fitbad the Tailor." Likewise the Haroun-al-Raschid of the modern Bagdad-on-the-Subway. The Editor-man, or more likely two or three of him, would be waiting for the promised (and in many cases already paid for) story, so Sydney Porter would say good-bye to the companions with whom he was sitting in a Broadway restaurant, proceed downtown, and stroll along the Bowery or adjacent streets until he fell in with the

* See "Whirligigs."

particular tramp who seemed most promising as copy. Sometimes he found the story and sometimes he did not. Often, when the idea came, it had absolutely nothing to do with the Bowery, or with tramps, or with two-cent coffee, or with anything remotely related thereto. But to Sydney Porter that was no reason for withholding the credit he considered due to the tramp. "He did not give me the idea," he once said in explanation, "but he did not drive it out of my head —which is just as important."

Whether the particular tramp of an evening's ramble meant the inked pages of a tale of Texas, or Central America, or New Orleans, O. Henry's wanderings about the East Side are reflected in some twenty or thirty stories with very definite backgrounds. The care with which Porter sought his local colour is indicated in The Sleuths,* in which a man from the Middle West goes to New York to find his sister. At her address he learns that she has moved away a month before, leaving no clue, and to help in the search he enlists the services of the famous detectives, Mullins & Shamrock Jolnes. The science of deduction leads to No. 12 Avenue C, which is described as an "old-fashioned brownstone house in a prosperous and respectable neighbourhood." Now, if any neighbourhood in New York City is not prosperous and respectable, it is that about Avenue C and Second Street. The Mulberry Bend of other years was hardly more unsightly and unkempt. O.

* See "Sixes and Sevens."

Henry had sensed its offensiveness through his eyes and his nostrils. The selection of the No. 12 was not mere chance. He knew that there was no such number: that on the southeast corner was a saloon bearing the number 10, and on the northeast corner the pharmacy was designated as No. 14. Just as there is no No. 13 Washington Square, there is no No. 12 Avenue C. Also there is no No. 162 Chilton Street, where the missing sister was eventually found, for the reason that in the Borough of Manhattan there is no Chilton Street at all.

Somewhere on the East Side is the famous Café Maginnis, where Ikey Snigglefritz, in the proudest, maddest moment of his life shook the hand of the great Billy McMahon. An indication as to the Café Maginnis's exact whereabouts is given in the information that Ikey, leaving it, "went down Hester Street, and up Chrystie and down Delancey" to where he lived. Ikey's home was in a crazy brick structure, "foul and awry," and there Cortlandt Van Duykinck found him and shook his hand, thereby completing the social triangle. There somewhere was the saloon of Dutch Mike where the Mulberry Hill gang and the Dry Dock gang met in the Homeric conflict the outcome of which sent Cork McManus to strange lands west of the Bowery and the adventures narrated in Past One at Rooney's.* There may be found the Second Avenue boarding-house where Miss Conway showed Andy Donovan the locket

* See "Strictly Business."

About New York With O. Henry 123

containing the portrait of her purely imaginary lover
(The Count and the Wedding Guest)*. Between the
Bowery and First Avenue, where the distance between
the two streets is the shortest, was the Blue Light Drug
Store, where Ikey Schoenstein † concocted the love
philtre that was to work the downfall of his rival,
Chunk Macgowan. In Orchard Street were the rooms
of the Give and Take Athletic Association where, as
told in The Coming Out of Maggie,‡ Tony Spinelli
played Prince Charming at the ball of the Clover Leaf
Social Club under the pseudonym of Terry O'Sullivan;
and farther up on the East Side, over against the elevated portion of the railroad, were the Beersheba Flats,
from which the variegated tenants were driven forth by
official edict to the grass of the park, and The City
of Dreadful Night.‡

IV

"HE SAW NO LONGER A RABBLE, BUT HIS BROTHERS
SEEKING THE IDEAL"

To look at the matter in its chronological aspect,
the first appearance of New York in the romance of
O. Henry was probably in the last part of "Cabbages
and Kings." There is a picture of two men sitting on
a stringer of a North River pier while a steamer from

* See "The Trimmed Lamp."
† See "The Four Million."
‡ See "The Voice of the City."

the tropics is unloading bananas and oranges. One of the men is O'Day, formerly of the Columbia Detective Agency. In a moment of confidence he tells his companion of the mistake which has brought him to his unenviable condition, and incidentally clears up for the reader the rather ugly mystery that throughout the book obscured the marriage of Frank Goodwin and the lady known in Coralio as Isabel Guilbert. To begin in another way, that is at the gateway of the city and of the new world, in the story The Lady Higher Up,* O. Henry pictures a dialogue between Mrs. Liberty, on her pedestal in the bay, and Miss Diana at the top of the tower of Madison Square Garden. Even the thick brogue which Mrs. Liberty has acquired cannot hide her envy of the other lady. In the matron's opinion Miss Diana has the best job for a statue in the whole town, with the Cat Show, and the Horse Show, and the military tournaments where the privates "look grand as generals, and the generals try to look grand as floorwalkers," and the Sportsman's Show, and above all, the French Ball "where the original Cohens and the Robert Emmet-Sangerbund Society dance the Highland Fling one with another."

But even before his first glimpse at Mrs. Liberty the visitor from a foreign shore has a sight of O. Henry's New York, as, from the deck of the transatlantic liner, the great wheels and towers of Coney Island are pointed out to him. Among these wheels and towers Alexander

* See "Sixes and Sevens."

Blinker, the owner of Brick Dust Row,* walked with Florence, his chance acquaintance of the boat, learned a lesson, and saw a light. No more was the jostling crowd a mass of vulgarians seeking gross joys. Counterfeit and false though the garish pleasures of the spangled temples were, he perceived that deep under the gilt surface they offered saving and apposite balm and satisfaction to the restless human heart. Here, at least, was the husk of Romance, the empty but shining casque of Chivalry, the breath-catching though safe-guarded dip and flight of Adventure. He saw no longer a rabble, but his brothers seeking the ideal. Again here, in the enchanted chicken coop of Madame Zozo, there was reading of Tobin's Palm,† and prophecies of a dark man and a light woman, of trouble and financial loss, of a voyage by water, and of a meeting with a man with a crooked nose. In The Greater Coney ‡ Dennis Carnahan expatiated ironically on the new city which has risen, Phœnix-like, out of the ashes of the old, and the wiping-out process, which, to his way of thinking, consisted of raising the price of admission from ten to twenty-five cents, and having a blonde named Maudie to take tickets instead of Micky, the Bowery Bite. The Babylonian towers and the Hindoo roof gardens blazing with lights, the camels moving with undulating walk, and the tawdry gondolas of artificial

* See "The Trimmed Lamp."
† See "The Four Million."
‡ See "Sixes and Sevens."

Venetian streets. These were what Mazie knew—
Mazie of A Lickpenny Lover.* These things her little
soul of a shop-girl saw when the millionaire painter-
traveller, Irving Carter, whose heart she had so
strangely won, proposed to her and drew his eloquent
picture of a honeymoon in lands beyond the seas.
These and no more. The next day her chum in the
store asks about her "swell friend." "Him," is the
retort. "Oh, he's a cheap skate. He ain't in it no
more. What do you suppose that guy wanted me to
do? He wanted me to marry him and go to Coney
Island for a wedding trip."

A Lickpenny Lover is just one of the stories in
which the specified location is not merely a scene of
the tale, but partly an explanation of it. For example,
the next time that the reader of these notes happens
to be at that point of New York City where Sixth
Avenue, Broadway, and Thirty-fourth Street meet, let
him recall Mammon and the Archer.† In that story
O. Henry is at his O. Henriest. Listen. The last
opportunity that the hero of the story, Richard Rock-
well, was to have to see Miss Lantry before her departure the next day for a two years' absence in Europe,
was to be in the hansom cab in which he was to take
her from the Grand Central Station to a box party at
Wallack's Theatre. His father, the old soap manufacturer, cheered him with expression of rough op-

* See "The Voice of the City."
† See "The Four Million."

timism and offered to back him with his money. His aunt gave him as an amulet his mother's wedding ring in wishing him Godspeed and success. Robert took the ring and started out on knightly quest. As the cab approached the crossing indicated the ring dropped tinkling to the pavement. In the few minutes' resulting delay the traffic assumed a tangled condition which held hero and heroine prisoners for hours, and late that night the boy's aunt went to the father with the news that the young people were engaged, and a warning that he should never boast of the power of money again, as the little gold band, an emblem of love and loyalty, had done what mere wealth could not accomplish. The story should have ended there, but with the characteristic touch, O. Henry introduced into the soap manufacturer's office the next morning a man who wore a red necktie and who answered to the name of Kelly. "Well," says the millionaire, "it was a pretty good bilin' of soap and how much do I owe you?" To which Kelly makes the reply that he has had five thousand dollars on account, that he had got the express wagons and cabs mostly for five dollars, but that the truckmen and motormen cost him ten dollars apiece, and the policemen twenty-five and fifty, "but," he adds enthusiastically, "when I got through I had a stage setting that would have made David Belasco envious. Why, a snake couldn't have got across Thirty-fourth Street."

V

SQUARES AND AVENUES

It is not likely that the Fourth Avenue of to-day would have had much to appeal to O. Henry's imagination. As it was half a dozen years ago it was one of his favourite thoroughfares, and reached its apotheosis in A Bird of Bagdad.* There O. Henry pictured it as a street that the city seemed to have forgotten in its growth, a street, born and bred in the Bowery, staggering northward full of good resolutions. At Fourteenth Street "it struts for a brief moment proudly in the glare of the museums and cheap theatres. It may yet become a fit mate for its highborn sister boulevard to the west, or its roaring, polyglot, broad-waisted cousin to the east." Then it passes what O. Henry in The Gold That Glittered,* called "the square presided over by George the Veracious," and comes to the silent and terrible mountains, buildings square as forts, high as the clouds, shutting out the sky, where thousands of slaves bend over desks all day. Next it glides into a mediæval solitude. On each side are the shops devoted to antiques. "Men in rusting armour stand in the windows and menace the hurrying cars with raised, rusty iron bumpers, hauberks, and helms, blunderbuses, Cromwellian breastplates, matchlocks, creeses, and the

* See "Strictly Business."

swords and daggers of an army of dead and gone gallants gleam dully in the ghostly light." This mediæval solitude forbodes an early demise. What street could live inclosed by these mortuary relics and trod by these spectral citizens? "Not Fourth Avenue. Not after the tinsel but enlivening glory of the Little Rialto—not after the echoing drum beats of Union Square. There need be no tears, ladies and gentlemen. 'Tis but the suicide of a street. With a shriek and a crash Fourth Avenue dives headlong into the tunnel at Thirty-fourth Street and is never seen again."

Three of the city squares, Madison Square, Union Square, and Gramercy Park play conspicuous parts in O. Henry's stories. His tales are full of human derelicts and where is there a more natural background for such than the public benches of these parks? He shows you the Bed Liners stamping their freezing feet, and the preacher standing on a pine box exhorting his transient and shifting audience. In this Bed Line were Walter Smuythe and the discharged coachman, Thomas McQuade, the night that the red motor car, humming up Fifth Avenue, lost its extra tire as narrated in The Fifth Wheel.* It was on a bench of the Square that the millionaire Pilkins found the penniless young eloping couple, Marcus Clayton of Roanoke County, Virginia, and Eva Bedford of Bedford County, of the same State. It was perhaps on the same bench that Soapy sat meditating just what violation of the law would in-

* See "Strictly Business."

sure his deportation to the hospitable purlieus of Blackwell's Island, which was his Palm Beach and Riviera for the winter months. It was near by at least that Prince Michael, of the Electorate of Valle Luna, known otherwise as Dopey Mike, looked up at the clock in the Metropolitan Tower and gave sage advice and consolation to the young man who was waiting to learn his fate as told in The Caliph, Cupid and the Clock.* While the auto with the white body and the red running gear was waiting near the corner of Twenty-sixth Street and Fifth Avenue, Parkenstacker made the acquaintance of the girl in gray and listened to the strange story born in the pages of Robert Louis Stevenson's "New Arabian Nights." Over on the sidewalk just in front of the Flatiron Building Sam Folwell and Cal Harkness, the Cumberland feudists, shooks hands Squaring the Circle.†

In following the trail of O. Henry's men and women through Madison Square you have the choice of many benches. This is not the case when Union Square is introduced in the story of Two Thanksgiving Day Gentlemen.‡ The writer tells you that when Stuffy Pete went to the Square to await the coming of the tall thin old gentleman dressed in black and wearing the old-fashioned kind of glasses that won't stay on the nose—the old gentleman who had been Stuffy's host

* See "The Four Million."
† See "The Voice of the City."
‡ See "The Trimmed Lamp."

every Thanksgiving Day for nine years—he "took his seat on the third bench to the right as you enter Union Square from the east, at the walk opposite the fountain." Across Union Square Hastings Beauchamp Moreley sauntered with a pitying look at the hundreds that lolled upon the park benches in The Assessor of Success.* One evening in the Square Murray and the dismissed police captain Marony were sitting side by side trying to think of schemes to repair their fallen fortunes. When opportunity came both acted According to Their Lights.* The captain was reduced to the point where, to use his own words, he would "marry the Empress of China for one bowl of chop suey, commit murder for a plate of beef stew, steal a wafer from a waif, or be a Mormon for a bowl of chowder." But his code of honour he still retained. He would not "squeal." It is to the other extreme of society that O. Henry takes us when he deals with Gramercy Park. All about that private square with its locked gates are the severe mansions of his aristocrats. There dwelt Alicia Van Der Pool before she married Robert Walmesley in The Defeat of the City.† A house facing the west side of the park was unquestionably the home of the Von der Ruyslings. That illustrious family had dwelt there for many years. In fact, in a spirit of obvious awe, O. Henry imparted the information that the Von der Ruyslings had received the first key ever

* See "The Trimmed Lamp."
† See "The Voice of the City."

made to Gramercy Park. In The Marry Month of May * we learn that near the Park old Mr. Coulson had a house, the gout, half a million dollars, a daughter, and a housekeeper. It was the daughter who thought to chill her father's springtime ardour by the introduction of a thousand pounds of ice into the basement. It was the housekeeper that thwarted the scheme, with the result that the old millionaire uttered his deferred proposal while Miss Van Meeker Constantia Coulson ran away with the iceman.

VI

GREENWICH VILLAGE

Of all men Sydney Porter was one of the most difficult of approach. To his last day he was shy and almost suspicious of the stranger who was not the casual stranger, that is, the acquaintance scraped in a mood on a bench in Madison Square, or Sheridan Park, or at some corner of "that thoroughfare which parallels and parodies Broadway." There was a little circle of his intimates consisting of such men as Richard Duffy, Gilman Hall, Robert H. Davis, H. Peyton Steger, Robert Rudd Whiting and a few more, to whom he was accessible at any hour of the night or day. But these men knew that it was out of the question to arrange formally a meeting between O. Henry and some one who wanted to know him; knew that at the first

* See "Whirligigs."

hint the quarry would take fright and disappear. So the encounter had to have every appearance of mere chance. Into Porter's rooms on Irving Place or in the Caledonia, where he lived later, the friend would drop, apparently for a word or two of business. With him there would be a stranger, whom the friend had chanced to pick up on the way. Nine times out of ten the friend would not introduce the other two. But after a few minutes' talk and in response to a prearranged signal, the stranger would remark that he had stumbled on a joint near the Bowery, or on upper Broadway, where there was a cocktail mixer who had tended bar in forty-seven cities of the United States. Before the words were out of his mouth Porter had reached for his hat. The friend was forgotten, and arm in arm story-spinner and stranger sallied forth into the night.

The bait thrown out was not always a cocktail mixer and his experiences. "The most picturesque bit of rear tenement that remains in New York." "That was the hint that I used when the nod came," one man who had found O. Henry in the manner suggested told the writer, "and in three minutes we were in the street. I led him down Irving Place to Fourteenth, to Sixth Avenue, past the Jefferson Market Police Court, into Greenwich Village, past Sheridan Park, and down Grove Street to the very end. There, between the front houses, Nos. 10 and 12, there is an opening. Beyond the opening is a triangle, in the middle of which is a tall telegraph pole, and at the back there are three old brick houses, the front windows of which look out diagonally at a wall against which leaves are growing. 'There is a story there,' said Porter, 'a story that suggests an episode in Murger's *Vie de Bohàme,* where the grisette at night waters the flowers to keep them alive. The lifetime of the flowers, you remember, was to be the lifetime of that transient love.' He wrote that story, I am sure, in The Last Leaf,* and when I see that bare, dreary yard, and the blank wall of the house twenty feet away, and the old ivy vine, I recall the pathetic tale of Sue and Joanna and the masterpiece that old Behrman painted at the cost of his life."

This Greenwich Village section of the city always appealed strongly to O. Henry's imagination. He liked to picture the odd zigzagging of the streets and to people them with the artists of his creation. Somewhere down in Greenwich Village was the "Vallambrosa" where the self-reliant Hetty lived and furnished the beef for the making of the Irish stew as related in The Third Ingredient.† There, too—in the red brick district, was The Furnished Room,‡ with its suggestion of mignonette. A few blocks away to the south and west is Abingdon Square. In The Thing's the Play,§ we are told "there stands a house near Abingdon

* See "The Trimmed Lamp."
† See "Options."
‡ See "The Four Million."
§ See "Strictly Business."

Square. On the ground floor there has been for twenty-five years a little store where toys and notions and stationery are sold." There Mrs. Frank Barry, deserted on her wedding night on account of a strange misunderstanding, lived out her life awaiting the return of her husband.

Fifth Avenue or First, Riverside Drive or Division Street, Broadway or the Bowery, Corlears Hook Park or Gramercy; no matter what the locality or the social scale of its denizens, it is always Bagdad. And with the night comes the glamour that belongs not to Arabia alone. In different masquerade the streets, bazaars, and walled houses of the Occidental city of romance are filled with the same kind of people that interested Haroun-al-Raschid in his golden prime. Clothes may be different, but underneath men and women are unchanged. With the eye of faith the traveller can see the Little Hunchback, Sinbad the Sailor, Fitbad the Tailor, the Beautiful Persian, the one-eyed Calenders, the Barber and his Six Brothers, and Ali Baba and Forty Robbers on every block.

Many have been the men and the women who have invaded New York as a literary field. But so far there has been but one conqueror of Alexander-like ambitions. And as became a conqueror, he was constantly re-christening the city to suit his own whimsical humour. At one moment it was his "Little Old Bagdad-on-the-Subway," at another, the "City of Too Many Caliphs"; at another, "Noisyville-on-the-Hudson"; or "The Big

Town of Razzle-Dazzle"; or, "Wolfville-on-the-Subway"; or, "The City of Chameleon Changes." Yet Porter discovered New York comparatively late in life; lived in it but the few brief last years. The story has often been told of how, a few minutes before the end came, he whispered to those about him: "Pull up the shades. I don't want to go home in the dark." I like to believe that he did not want to go home without one last glimpse of the town that he had learned to love so well; one last glimpse of his "Little Old Bagdad-on-the-Subway"; his "City of Too Many Caliphs."

O. HENRY AND NEW ORLEANS

By Caroline Francis Richardson

A SETTING that appealed strongly both to O. Henry's story-instinct and to his sympathy was downtown New Orleans. Like many other writers he found inspiration in the narrow, dingy, shadowy Quarter whose buildings and street names and traditions tell of many things that to-day are lost: riches and lives and causes. But O. Henry used his "copy" differently from other story-tellers who have found suggestion in New Orleans. In the O. Henry tales no plot hinges on a mixture of blood; no hero or heroine is engulfed by flood or devoured by plague; no person speaks an unintelligible dialect. There is no use of Mardi Gras, All Saints' Day, or *quatorze juillet*. And this handling of material is quite characteristic of the author. In all his stories, wherever placed, he makes use of every detail that will add reality to a character or an occurrence. But he does not introduce localities and localisms merely for their intrinsic interest.

As a setting New Orleans can claim but a scant share in the lives of some of O. Henry's knights of high adventure. This is the case with a certain grafter and his partner, Caligula, who of their stay could remember only some drinks "invented by the creoles during the period of Louey Cans, in which they are still served at the side doors"; and an attempt "to make the French Quarter pay up the back trading stamps due on the Louisiana Purchase." It is in that story, Hostages to Momus,* that the Grafter explains the component parts of a perfect breakfast: "There'll never be a perfect breakfast eaten until some man grows arms long enough to stretch down to New Orleans for his coffee and over to Norfolk for his rolls, and reaches up to Vermont and digs a slice of butter out of a spring-house, and then turns over a beehive close to a clover patch out in Indiana for the rest. Then he'd come pretty close to making a meal that the gods eat on Mount Olympus."

Many of these birds of passage merely arrive and depart by way of fruit steamers coming from or going to an explosion in Central America. In that case, the city sees them only while they pick their way over a banana-strewn wharf, dodging the long line of men who pass the green bunches in a swaying chain from the hold of the ship to the freight cars near by. It was by pretending to be a part of such a line that the too sympathetic, too easily won Clancy and the escaping revolutionist, General de Vega, landed undetected from the ship in which they had travelled as stowaways (The Shamrock and the Palm†). In Lafayette Square

* See "The Gentle Grafter."
† See "Cabbages and Kings."

O. Henry and New Orleans

Clancy consummated his dark scheme. With the connivance of a policeman, a fellow Irishman, the General was arrested as a vagrant and sentenced to sixty days' hard labour. The General, be it remembered, had lured Clancy to Guatemala as a revolutionist, but had forced him to assist for sixty days in building a railroad. And now—"Havin' no money, they set him (The General) to work his fine out with a gang from the parish prison clearing Ursulines Street. Around the corner was a saloon decorated genially with electric fans and cool merchandise. I made that me headquarters, and every fifteen minutes I'd walk around and take a look at the little man filibustering with a rake and shovel. . . . Carrambos. Erin go bragh!"

In Phœbe * a less triumphant Irishman is shown us: "Bad-luck Kearney." His untoward adventures reach us through Captain Patricio Maloné, "a Hiberno-Iberian creole," who tells the story while sitting over cognac in a "little red-tiled café near Congo Square." From his first sight of Kearney falling into a cellar on Tchoupitoulas Street, the Captain should have taken warning. But though Kearney conscientiously declares his handicap, even leading his new friend out into the middle of the great width of Canal Street in order to point out the sinister Saturn and the evil satellite, Phœbe, under which he, Kearney, was born, Captain Maloné refuses to yield to superstition. Later, however, circumstances oblige him to admit the power of

* See "Roads of Destiny."

the stars, and for the good of the cause, they part. The Captain's conversion is confirmed by his meeting with Kearney a year afterward. On this final occasion Captain Maloné, walking near Poydras Market, is brushed aside by "an immensely stout, pink-faced lady in black satin." . . . "Behind her trailed a little man laden to the gunwale with bundles and bags of goods and vegetables." And the little man calls conciliatingly, "I'm coming, Phœbe!"

Very rarely do historic buildings slip into these stories, so it is only as a measure of distance that the old Bourbon Street opera house is used. In A Matter of Mean Elevation,* the reader learns that "The Carabobo Indians are easily the most enthusiastic lovers of music between the equator and the French Opera House in New Orleans." In Blind Man's Holiday,* too, there are buildings we might see on a post card: "the Rue Chartres perishes in the old Place d'Armes. The ancient Cabildo, where Spanish justice fell like hail, faces it, and the Cathedral, another provincial ghost, overlooks it. Its centre is a little iron-railed park. . . . Pedestalled high above it, the general sits his cavorting steed."

In the same story O. Henry makes another departure and yields to the sentiment of French Town: "The Rue Chartres, in New Orleans, is a street of ghosts. It lies in the quarter where the Frenchman in his prime set up translated pride and glory; where, also, the

* See "Whirligigs."

arrogant don had swaggered, and dreamed of gold grants and ladies' gloves. Every flagstone has its grooves worn by footsteps going royally to the wooing and the fighting. Every house has a princely heartbreak; each doorway its untold tale of gallant promise and slow decay. By night the Rue Chartres is now but a murky fissure, from which the groping wayfarer sees, flung up against the sky, the tangled filigree of Moorish balconies. The old houses of monsieur stand yet, indomitable against the century, but their essence is gone. The street is one of ghosts to whosoever can see them." And in this story is O. Henry's one use of a New Orleans festival: it is on Carnival costumes that Norah Greenway works every and all night—Norah Greenway, the girl who fabricates a past so that her lover, a self-confessed sinner, may have the courage to ask her to marry him.

O. Henry's philosophers of Fortune usually shun hotels. An emphasized instance is that of William Trotter (Helping the Other Fellow[*]) who comes to New Orleans after a long stay in Aguas Frescas. His brother has offered him a position at a salary of five thousand a year, and expects to meet him at the St. Charles Hotel where they will discuss details. "When I arrived at the Crescent City, I hurried away—far away from St. Charles to a dim *chambre garnie* in Bienville Street. And there, looking down from my attic window from time to time at the old absinthe house

[*] See "Rolling Stones."

across the street, I wrote this story to buy my bread and butter."

And it was in "one of those rare old hostelries in Royal Street" that Monsieur Morin lodged—the Monsieur Morin who is so important though unseen a figure in "Cherchez la Femme."* The search for the lady is the self-assumed responsibility of two reporters: Robbins, of the *Picayune*, and Dumars, of *L'Abeille*, "the old French newspaper that has buzzed for nearly a century." In a café in Dumaine Street they argue and conjecture as to M. Morin's disposition of Madame Thibault's twenty thousand dollars, of which he had had the care. The money is finally found in the shape of government bonds carefully pasted by Madame Thibault herself over the unsightly cracks in the wall of one of her rear rooms.

Another native protagonist, in The Renaissance of Charleroi,* is Grandemont Charles, "a little creole gentleman, aged thirty-four, with a bald spot on the top of his head and the manners of a prince. By day he was a clerk in a cotton broker's office in one of those cold, rancid mountains of oozy brick, down near the levee. By night, in the old French Quarter, he was again the last male descendant of the Charles family." And in this last character he determines to spend his painfully saved hoard of six hundred dollars in a renaissance of past glories. He secures the use of the old plantation house, Charleroi; he fills it with appropriate furniture,

* See "Roads of Destiny."

O. Henry and New Orleans 143

rented from the antique shops in Royal and Chartres streets; he orders wines and food from famous places —and for an evening, Charleroi lives again. That no one of his invited guests appears, that an uninvited guest does appear, whose presence means more to Grandemont than even the glorious past—all this makes it an O. Henry story.

A plantation below the city is the setting for a climax in Whistling Dick's Christmas Stocking.* By means of a freight-car Dick arrives in the "big, almsgiving, long-suffering city of the South, the cold weather paradise of tramps." After a cautious survey that includes the levee "pimpled with dark bulks of merchandise," the long line of Algiers across the river, the tugs, the ferries, and the Italian luggers, Dick climbs warily down and starts, whistling, toward Lafayette Square to meet a pal. But a friendly policeman warns Dick of a new and inhospitable city ordinance, and he departs hastily for the open road. A stall keeper in the French Market gives him breakfast, and he is almost happy until Chalmette, with its "vast and bewildering industry," frightens him and drives him along a country road hemmed in on one side by the high green levee and on the other by a mysterious, frog-haunted, mosquito-infested marsh. The incident of a tramp saving a family from burglary and fire, because of a kindly word from a young girl, is not new; and the plantation house and household are typical and trite.

* See "The Roads of Destiny."

But Whistling Dick is real. It is entirely logical that after his glorious evening as honoured guest, and his comfortable night on the floor of his well-furnished room, he should, on looking out of the window at the dawn of Christmas Day, feel a distinct shock. He sees and hears the evidences of the labour that a monster sugar crop has forced upon a part even of the world holiday. "Here was a poem; an epic—nay, a tragedy —with work, the curse of the world, for its theme." A few moments later Whistling Dick, carefree and happy, strolls along the top of the levee, away from his grateful hosts, away into the new day and the untrammelled life.

"A YANKEE MAUPASSANT"

A Summary of the Criticism of Ten Years Ago

EVERY reader of current American newspapers and magazines is familiar with the name "O. Henry." It is a pen name, concealing the identity of Mr. Sydney Porter, the author of sundry books of short stories. For some time now his reputation has been steadily growing. Throughout the country are people of all sorts and conditions who agree enthusiastically on one point—that no one else can write short stories like O. Henry's. The critics were at first slow to accept his work. The suggestion that he was "a Yankee Maupassant," * came from his publishers, and did not, for a while, impress the writing fraternity. But now the tables are completely turned. We find William Marion Reedy, of the St. Louis *Mirror*, affirming that, to his thinking, Mr. Porter deserves the very flattering designation conferred upon him; and Henry James Forman, of the editorial staff of the *North American Review*,

---

* This appellation is an unconscious tribute to the broad Americanism of a man who lived most of his life in North Carolina and Texas.

declares: "He writes with the skill of a Maupassant, and a humour Maupassant never dreamed of." The *Bookman* says, editorially:

"While we are inclined to be conservative in the matter of estimating a contemporary writer, and find exceedingly exasperating these impulsive and extravagant recognitions of 'new Stevensons' and 'new Kiplings,' and 'new de Maupassants' and 'American Dickenses,' the time is past for any restraint in the frank appreciation of the work of the author who signs himself 'O. Henry.' The man is in many respects an extraordinary workman and a consummate artist."

The distinguishing characteristics of O. Henry's work are his journalistic style and his democratic instinct. The two combine, as Francis Hackett, the literary editor of the Chicago *Evening Post* points out, in what is distinctly "an original revelation of life." Mr. Hackett says:

"O. Henry writes with a glitter that is characteristic half of the New York *Sun*, half of the *Smart Set*. . . . His scope is restricted. His manner is not discursive. He gets sensational contrasts and assertive colouring into each short story. Allowing for this, he gives us a humorous yet profound understanding of a phase that has not yet been treated before in American art, gives us intimacy with an order of metropolitan characters and circumstances not likely to be better focussed or illumined in our generation.

"O. Henry accepts, with a mixture of irony, wit, and

"A Yankee Maupassant" 147

sympathy, the distressing fact that a human being can be a clerk, the remarkable fact that a clerk can be a human being. He knows the clerk, knows him in his works and pomps. But there is a peculiarity in O. Henry's attitude toward the clerk. . . . Most literary men are intrenched in culture, obfuscated by it. They take the uncultured morosely or pityingly or mordantly. They discuss those who are not 'élite' as a physician would discuss a case—scientifically, often humanly, interested, but always with a strong sense of the case's defects and deficiencies.

"To O. Henry, on the contrary, the clerk is neither abnormal nor subnormal. He writes of him without patronizing him. He realizes the essential and stupendous truth that to himself the clerk is not pitiable. He takes into account, in other words, the adjustments that every man makes to constitute himself the apex of this sphere—for, after all, there are 800,000,000 apices on this sphere, if we dare to assume that fowl and fishes are not also self-conscious and self-centred.

"When one says 'clerk' one means $15-a-week humanity. O. Henry has specialized in this humanity with loving care, with a Kiplingesque attention to detail. But his is far from the humourless method of Gissing and Merrick, who were no more happy in a boarding-house than Thoreau would have been in the Waldorf-Astoria. O. Henry never forgets the inherent, the unconscious humour in the paradoxes and contrasts of mixed civilization, the crudities of which serve only to exasperate the misplaced and morbid. He is no moral paradoxist, like Shaw, no soured idealist, like Zola, no disgruntled esthete, like Gissing. It is the comedy of the paradoxes and contrasts that he searches and displays—a comedy in which he miraculously keeps the balance, often by the adventitious aid of irony and satire, not sacrificing the clerk to the man of culture, nor, on the other hand, losing perspective in magnifying the clerk."

But O. Henry does not confine himself to the clerk. As Mr. Hackett tells us:

"In one sense Broadway is the spinal column of his art, and the nerve branches cover all Manhattan. He knows the side streets where Mamie boards. He knows Harlem. He knows the narrow-chested flat. He knows the Bowery, Irish and Yiddish. He knows the Tenderloin, cop, panhandler, man about town, sport, bartender, and waiter. He knows Shanley's and Childs's, the lemon-odoured buffet and the French table d'hôte. He knows the sham Bohemia, the real Bohemia. And his stories are starred with little vignettes of the town, paragraphs of unostentatious art that let us see Madison Square, or the White Way, or the Park (over and over again the Park), or the side street in springtime—all clear as the vision in the crystal.

"O. Henry's triumphs are often triumphs of fancy. He has the sense of the marvellous which belongs to tellers of the short story since the nights of Arabia. And O. Henry can discover in Manhattan the wonder of fable and adventure, the eternal symbols of imagination, the beauty of the jewel in the toad."

To this should be added the tribute of William Marion Reedy:

"As a depicter of the life of New York's four million—club men, fighters, thieves, policemen, touts, shopgirls, lady cashiers, hoboes, actors, stenographers, and what not—O. Henry has no equal for keen insight into the beauties and meannesses of character or motive. Mordant though he be at times his heart is with innocence and right, but he sees the fun that underlies sophistication and selfishness. Not only does he see life, but he sees its problems and in a certain shy-sly way suggests his solutions therefor. His gifts of description are of a surprising variety in method. His pictures, mostly small, intimate greater scopes and deeper vistas. Afraid of pathos, his very promptness to avoid it upon its slightest hint of imminence gives poignancy to the note he thus strikes as by suggestion. He loves the picaroon and the vagabond, and dowers them with vocabularies rich and strange and fanciful. . . . He always has a story. The style or the mood may lure you away from it momentarily, but the tale always asserts its primacy, and its end comes always in just the whimsical way you didn't expect. O. Henry is inexhaustible in quip, in imagery, in quick, sharp, spontaneous invention. In his apparent carelessness we suspect a carefulness, but this is just wherein he is sib to the French short-story writers, chief among them de Maupassant. Della Cruscan critics may disapprove of him for his slang, but until you know his slang, you never know what a powerful vehicle slang can be in the hands of one who can mate it with the echoes from and essences of true literary expression. It is not the slang of George Ade, or Henry M. Blossom, or George V. Hobart. Henry's slang has some of the savour that we find in the archaic vocabulary invented for himself by Chatterton. Its content transcends the capacity of the mere argot of the street. In the American short story to-day O. Henry has demonstrated himself a delightful master, one absolutely unapproachable in swift visualization and penetrative interpretation of life, as any and all of the books now to his credit will show to any one capable of understanding."

O. HENRY'S SHORT STORIES

By Henry James Forman

MR. SYDNEY PORTER, the gentleman who, in the language of some of his characters, is "denounced" by the euphonious pen name of O. Henry, has breathed new life into the short story. Gifted as he is with a flashing wit, abundant humour, and quick observation, no subject has terrors for him. If it be too much to say, in the old phrase, that nothing human is alien to him, at least the larger part of humanity is his domain. The very title of one of his books, "The Four Million," is a protest against those who believe that New York contains only four hundred people worth while. O. Henry backs the census-taker against the social arbiter. The rich and the fashionable are, in his tales, conceived much in the spirit of similar characters in melodrama, except that the ingredient of humour is put in to mitigate them. Indeed, they figure but seldom. But the poor and the lowly, the homeless lodger of the city park, the vagabond of the "bread line," the waitress, the shop and factory girl, the ward politician, the city policeman, the whole "ruck and rabble" of life, so meaningless to the comfortable, unobservant bourgeois, are set forth always with keen knowledge, with a laughing humour, and not infrequently with a tender, smiling pathos. As this panorama of the undenoted faces of the great city passes before the reader, he becomes his own Caliph Haroun-al-Raschid, and New York a teeming Bagdad, full of romance and mystery.

The facility, the light touch of O. Henry, his mastery of the vernacular, his insight into the life of the disinherited, make it needless for him to resort to such inventions as Stevenson's learned Arabian, imaginary author of the "New Arabian Nights." The piquant and picturesque phrasing, the dash of slang, the genial and winning fancy seem to carry off the most fantastic situations. The Touchstone, the jester, the merrymaker has always enjoyed a certain license if he had but the wit not to abuse it. O. Henry's fun is never of the slapstick variety and his pathos never bathos. We are shaken with sad laughter at the many and divers attempts of the park-bench vagabond, Soapy,* to be arrested and sent to the workhouse for the winter months. He eats a meal and does not pay, he steals an umbrella, he accosts unescorted women, but all to no purpose. The police seem to regard him "as a king who could do no wrong." But as he passes by a church the organ music of an anthem vividly recalls his boyhood, stirs the tramp to his depths, and he resolves to turn over a new leaf. He will seek work and be a man. Then the policeman lays a hand upon him, hales him before a magistrate as a vagrant, and the city's swirl-

* The Cop and the Anthem, in "The Four Million."

ing machinery of the law sends Soapy to "the Island" after all. And the author smiles with tender compassion over this poor shuttlecock of fate.

With no less humorous kindness does he deal with 'Tildy, "the unwooed drudge," the plain little waitress in an Eighth Avenue chop-house.* All the hurrying *clientèle* of that eating-house admired Aileen, who "was tall, beautiful, lively, gracious, and learned in persiflage." But no one had a word for 'Tildy of the freckles and the hay-coloured hair, until one day a tipsy laundry clerk put his arm round 'Tildy's waist and kissed her. For a brief space that transformed her life. 'Tildy the unnoticed began to bind ribbons in her hair, to prink and to preen after the fashion of daughters of Eve. "A gentleman insulted me to-day," she modestly informed all her customers. "He put his arm around my waist and kissed me." And as the diners turned upon her the stream of badinage hitherto directed at Aileen alone, 'Tildy's heart swelled in her bosom, "for she saw at last the towers of Romance rise above the horizon of the gray plain in which she had for so long travelled." 'Tildy had a thrilling sensation of fear lest Seeders, the laundry clerk, in a mood of jealous love-madness, rush in and shoot her with a pistol. This she deplored, for no one had shot Aileen for love, and she did not wish to overshadow her friend. When Seeders does come in it is only to apologize, with the plea that he was tipsy.

* The Brief Début of Tildy, in "The Four Million."

'Tildy's towers of romance crumble to earth. The glory fades suddenly, for it was not love at all that actuated Seeders. But Aileen the staunch-hearted comforts 'Tildy in her sorrow, for if Seeders "were any kind of a gentleman," she tells her, "he wouldn't of apologized."

"The Trimmed Lamp" is of a piece with "The Four Million," filled with the tragi-comedy of life much as it appeared to Dickens and to François Villon. In "Heart of the West" the author exploits a vein many have attempted in a short story as well as in the novel —the so-called "wild West." But no one, it is safe to say, has brought so much fun and humour to the Western story. Cattle-king, cowboy, miner, the plains and the chaparral—material of the "dime novel," but all treated with the skill of a Maupassant, and a humour Maupassant never dreamed of. The merest sketch of them has a certain substance to it. Yet it is idle to compare O. Henry with anybody. No talent could be more original or more delightful. The combination of technical excellence with whimsical, sparkling wit, abundant humour, and a fertile invention is so rare that the reader is content without comparisons.

O. HENRY INDEX

A

ACCORDING TO THEIR LIGHTS. *See:* Trimmed Lamp, The.
ADJUSTMENT OF NATURE, AN. *See:* Four Million, The.
ADMIRAL, THE. *See:* Cabbages and Kings.
ADVENTURES IN NEURASTHENIA. *Same as* Let Me Feel Your Pulse.
ADVENTURES OF SHAMROCK JOLNES, THE. *See:* Sixes and Sevens.
AFTER THE BATTLE. *Same as* The Crucible.
AFTER TWENTY YEARS. *See:* Four Million, The.
AFTERNOON MIRACLE, AN. *See:* Heart of the West.
ALIAS JIMMY VALENTINE. *Dramatization of* Retrieved Reformation, A.
APOLOGY, AN. *See:* Rolling Stones.
ARISTOCRACY VERSUS HASH. *See:* Rolling Stones.
ART AND THE BRONCO. *See:* Roads of Destiny.
ASSESSOR OF SUCCESS, THE. *See:* Trimmed Lamp, The.
AT ARMS WITH MORPHEUS. *See:* Sixes and Sevens.
ATAVISM OF JOHN TOM LITTLE BEAR, THE. *See:* Rolling Stones.
ATWOOD, JOHNNY. *See:* Note under Cabbages and Kings.

B

BABES IN THE JUNGLE. *See:* Strictly Business.
BADGE OF POLICEMAN O'ROON, THE. *See:* Trimmed Lamp, The.
BEST-SELLER. *See:* Options.

O. Henry Index

BETWEEN ROUNDS. *See:* Four Million, The.
BEXAR SCRIP, NO. 2692. *See:* Rolling Stones.
BIRD OF BAGDAD, A. *See:* Strictly Business.
BLACKJACK BARGAINER, A. *See:* Whirligigs.
BLIND MAN'S HOLIDAY. *See:* Whirligigs.
BRICKDUST ROW. *See:* Trimmed Lamp, The.
BRIEF DÉBUT OF 'TILDY, THE. *See:* Four Million, The.
BURIED TREASURE. *See:* Options.
BUYER FROM CACTUS CITY, THE. *See:* Trimmed Lamp, The.
BY COURIER. *See:* Four Million, The.

C

CABALLERO'S WAY, THE. *See:* Heart of the West.
CABBAGES AND KINGS.

The stories in this volume, though apparently disconnected chapters, fall into four main groups, with the exception of one independent tale, The Lotus and the Bottle. But the stories all have a loose inter-relation owing to the fact that Coralio in Central America is their common stage, and that the *dramatis personæ*, generally speaking, is the same throughout. For the advantage of readers who wish to get the chapters of the various stories in their natural order, the groups are here marked alphabetically. For instance, all the chapters centring about Frank Goodwin are grouped with The Money Maze as A. Those about Johnny Atwood with Cupid's Exile Number Two as B. Those about Keogh and Clancy with The Phonograph and the Graft as C. Those about Dicky as D and those about The Admiral as E.

CONTENTS:

The Proem: By the Carpenter, A
"Fox-in-the-Morning," A
The Lotus and the Bottle
The Phonograph and the Graft, C
Money Maze, A
The Admiral, E
The Flag Paramount, E
The Shamrock and the Palm, C
The Remnants of the Code, A
Smith, A
Caught, A
Cupid's Exile Number Two, B
Shoes, B

Ships, B
Masters of Arts, C
Dicky, D
Rouge et Noir, D
Two Recalls, A
The Vitagraphoscope, A-C

CACTUS, THE. *See:* Waifs and Strays.
CALIPH AND THE CAD, THE. *See:* Sixes and Sevens.
CALIPH, CUPID AND THE CLOCK, THE. *See:* Four Million, The.
CALL LOAN, A. *See:* Heart of the West.
CALL OF THE TAME, THE. *See:* Strictly Business.
CALLOWAY'S CODE. *See:* Whirligigs.
CARTOONS BY O. HENRY. *See:* Rolling Stones.
CASE OF DIANA'S HUSBAND, THE. *Same as:* Defeat of the City, The.
CAUGHT. *See:* Cabbages and Kings.
CENTRAL AMERICA, STORIES OF. *See:* Locality.
CHAIR OF PHILANTHROMATHEMATICS, THE. *See:* Gentle Grafter, The.
CHAMPION OF THE WEATHER, THE. *See:* Sixes and Sevens.
CHAPARRAL CHRISTMAS GIFT, A. *See:* Whirligigs.
CHAPARRAL PRINCE, A. *See:* Heart of the West.
"CHERCHEZ LA FEMME." *See:* Roads of Destiny.
CHRISTMAS BY INJUNCTION. *See:* Heart of the West.
CHURCH WITH AN OVERSHOT WHEEL, THE. *See:* Sixes and Sevens.
CITY OF DREADFUL NIGHT, THE. *See:* Voice of the City, The.
CLARION CALL, THE. *See:* Voice of the City, The.
COMEDY IN RUBBER, A. *See:* Voice of the City, The.
COMING-OUT OF MAGGIE, THE. *See:* Four Million, The.
COMPLETE LIFE OF JOHN HOPKINS, THE. *See:* Voice of the City, The.
COMPLIMENTS OF THE SEASON. *See:* Strictly Business.
CONFESSIONS OF A HUMOURIST. *See:* Waifs and Strays.
CONSCIENCE IN ART. *See:* Gentle Grafter, The.
COP AND THE ANTHEM, THE. *See:* Four Million, The.
COSMOPOLITE IN A CAFÉ, A. *See:* Four Million, The.

COUNT AND THE WEDDING GUEST, THE. *See:* Trimmed Lamp, The.
COUNTRY OF ELUSION, THE. *See:* Trimmed Lamp, The.
CUPID À LA CARTE. *See:* Heart of the West.
CUPID'S EXILE NUMBER TWO. *See:* Cabbages and Kings.

D

DAY RESURGENT, THE. *See:* Strictly Business.
DAY WE CELEBRATE, THE. *See:* Sixes and Sevens.
DEFEAT OF THE CITY, THE. *See:* Voice of the City, The.
DEPARTMENTAL CASE, A. *See:* Roads of Destiny.
DETECTIVE DETECTOR, THE. *See:* Waifs and Strays.
DIAMOND OF KALI, THE. *See:* Sixes and Sevens.
DICKY. *See:* Cabbages and Kings.
DINNER AT——, A. *See:* Rolling Stones.
DINNER FOR TWO, A. *Same as* Madison Square Arabian Night, A.
DISCOUNTERS OF MONEY, THE. *See:* Roads of Destiny.
DOG AND THE PLAYLET. *See:* Waifs and Strays.
DOOR OF UNREST, THE. *See:* Sixes and Sevens.
DOUBLE DECEIVER, A. *Dramatization of* Double-Dyed Deceiver, A.
DOUBLE-DYED DECEIVER, A. *See:* Roads of Destiny.
DOUGHERTY'S EYE-OPENER. *See:* Voice of the City, The.
DREAM, THE. *See:* Rolling Stones.
DUEL, THE. *See:* Strictly Business.
DUPLICITY OF HARGRAVES, THE. *See:* Sixes and Sevens.

E

EAST SIDE TRAGEDY, AN: "THE GUILTY PARTY." *See:* Trimmed Lamp, The.
EASTER OF THE SOUL, THE. *See:* Voice of the City, The.
ELSIE IN NEW YORK. *See:* Trimmed Lamp, The.
EMANCIPATION OF BILLY, THE. *See:* Roads of Destiny.
ENCHANTED KISS, THE. *See:* Roads of Destiny.

ENCHANTED PROFILE, THE. *See:* Roads of Destiny.
ETHICS OF PIG, THE. *See:* Gentle Grafter, The.
EXACT SCIENCE OF MATRIMONY, THE. *See:* Gentle Grafter, The.
EXTRADITED FROM BOHEMIA. *See:* Voice of the City, The.

F

FAIRY OF UNFULFILMENT, THE. *Same as* Ferry of Unfulfilment, The.
FERRY OF UNFULFILMENT, THE. *See:* Trimmed Lamp, The.
FICKLE FORTUNE, OR HOW GLADYS HUSTLED. *See:* Rolling Stones.
FIFTH WHEEL, THE. *See:* Strictly Business.
FLAG PARAMOUNT, THE. *See:* Cabbages and Kings.
FOG IN SANTONE, A. *See:* Rolling Stones.
FOOL-KILLER, THE. *See:* Voice of the City, The.
FOREIGN POLICY OF COMPANY 99, THE. *See:* Trimmed La p, The.
FOUR MILLION, THE—SHORT STORIES.

CONTENTS:

- Tobin's Palm
- The Gift of the Magi
- A Cosmopolite in a Café
- Between Rounds
- The Cop and the Anthem
- An Adjustment of Nature
- Memoirs of a Yellow Dog
- The Love-Philtre of Ikey Schoenstein
- Mammon and the Archer
- Springtime à la Carte
- The Green Door
- From the Cabby's Seat
- An Unfinished Story
- The Skylight Room
- A Service of Love
- The Coming-Out of Maggie
- Man About Town
- The Caliph, Cupid and the Clock
- Sisters of the Golden Circle
- The Romance of a Busy Broker
- After Twenty Years
- Lost on Dress Parade
- By Courier
- The Furnished Room
- The Brief Début of 'Tildy

FOUR ROSES, THE—VERSE. *See:* Roses, Ruses, and Romance in Voice of the City, The.
FOURTH IN SALVADOR, THE. *See:* Roads of Destiny.

"Fox-in-the-Morning." *See:* Cabbages and Kings.
Friendly Call, The. *See:* Rolling Stones.
Friends in San Rosario. *See:* Roads of Destiny.
From Each According to His Ability. *See:* Voice of the City, The.
From the Cabby's Seat. *See:* Four Million, The.
Furnished Room, The. *See:* Four Million, The.

G

Gentle Grafter, The (Illustrated)—Short Stories.

CONTENTS:

- The Octopus Marooned
- Jeff Peters as a Personal Magnet
- Modern Rural Sports
- The Chair of Philanthromathematics
- The Hand that Riles the World
- The Exact Science of Matrimony
- A Midsummer Masquerade
- Shearing the Wolf
- Innocents of Broadway
- Conscience in Art
- The Man Higher Up
- A Tempered Wind
- Hostages to Momus
- The Ethics of Pig

Georgia's Ruling. *See:* Whirligigs.
Ghost of a Chance, The. *See:* Sixes and Sevens.
Gift of the Magi, The. (*To be dramatized*). *See:* Four Million, The.
Gift of the Wise Men, The. *Same as* Gift of the Magi, The.
"Girl." *See:* Whirligigs.
Girl and the Graft, The. *See:* Strictly Business.
Girl and the Habit, The. *See:* Strictly Business.
Gold that Glittered, The. *See:* Strictly Business.
Goodwin, Frank. *See:* Note under Cabbages and Kings.
Greater Coney, The. *See:* Sixes and Sevens.
Green Door, The. (*Has been dramatized.*) *See:* Four Million, The.
Guardian of the Accolade, The. *See:* Roads of Destiny.

GUARDIAN OF THE 'SCUTCHEON. *Same as* Guardian of the Accolade.

"GUILTY PARTY"—AN EAST SIDE TRAGEDY, THE. *See:* Trimmed Lamp, The.

GUTHRIE WOOING, A. *Same as* Cupid à la Carte.

H

HALBERDIER OF THE LITTLE RHEINSCHLOSS, THE. *See:* Roads of Destiny.

HAND THAT RILES THE WORLD, THE. *See:* Gentle Grafter, The.

HANDBOOK OF HYMEN, THE. *See:* Heart of the West.

HARBINGER, THE. *See:* Voice of the City, The.

HARLEM TRAGEDY, A. *See:* Trimmed Lamp, The.

HE ALSO SERVES. *See:* Options.

HEAD-HUNTER, THE. *See:* Options.

HEART OF THE WEST—SHORT STORIES.

CONTENTS:

Hearts and Crosses
The Ransom of Mack
Telemachus, Friend
The Handbook of Hymen
The Pimienta Pancakes
Seats of the Haughty
Hygeia at the Solito
An Afternoon Miracle
The Higher Abdication
Cupid à la Carte
The Caballero's Way
The Sphinx Apple
The Missing Chord
A Call Loan
The Princess and the Puma
The Indian Summer of Dry Valley Johnson
Christmas by Injunction
A Chaparral Prince
The Reformation of Calliope

HEARTS AND CROSSES. *See:* Heart of the West.

HEARTS AND HANDS. *See:* Waifs and Strays.

HELPING THE OTHER FELLOW. *See:* Rolling Stones.

HIDING OF BLACK BILL, THE. *See:* Options.

HIGHER ABDICATION, THE. *See:* Heart of the West.

HIGHER PRAGMATISM, THE. *See:* Options.

HIM WHO WAITS, TO. *See:* Options.

HOLDING UP A TRAIN. *See:* Sixes and Sevens.

HOSTAGES TO MOMUS. *See:* Gentle Grafter, The.

How Gladys Hustled, or "Fickle Fortune." *See:* Rolling Stones.
Hygeia at the Solito. *See:* Heart of the West.
Hypotheses of Failure, The. (*Basis of a vaudeville sketch.*) *See:* Whirligigs.

I

"I Go to Seek on Many Roads,"—Verse—Heading of Roads of Destiny. *See:* Roads of Destiny.
Ikey Schoenstein, The Love Philtre of. *See:* Four Million, The.
Indian Summer of Dry Valley Johnson, The. *See:* Heart of the West.
Innocents of Broadway. *See:* Gentle Grafter, The.

J

Jeff Peters as a Personal Magnet. *See:* Gentle Grafter, The.
Jeff Peters Stories.

See: The Gentle Grafter; Cupid à la Carte (*In* Heart of the West); and The Atavism of John Tom Little Bear (*In* Rolling Stones).

Jimmie Hayes and Muriel. *See:* Sixes and Sevens.
Jimmy Samson. *English dramatic version of* A Retrieved Reformation.
John Hopkins, The Complete Life of. *See:* Voice of the City, The.
John Tom Little Bear, The Atavism of. *See:* Rolling Stones.
Johnny Atwood. *See:* Note under Cabbages and Kings.

K

Katy of Frogmore Flats. *Same as* The Pendulum.
Keogh and Clancy. *See:* Note under Cabbages and Kings.

L

LADY HIGHER UP, THE. *See:* Sixes and Sevens.
LAST LEAF, THE. *See:* Trimmed Lamp, The.
LAST OF THE TROUBADOURS, THE. *See:* Sixes and Sevens.
LAW AND ORDER. *See:* Sixes and Sevens.
"LAZY SHEPHERDS, SEE YOUR LAMBKINS"—DAVID'S VERSE IN ROADS OF DESTINY. *See:* Roads of Destiny.
LET ME FEEL YOUR PULSE. *See:* Sixes and Sevens.

> Also issued separately as a small illustrated book. This story is largely based upon O. Henry's own ill-fated search for health.

LETTERS FROM O. HENRY. *See:* Rolling Stones.

> Two to Gilman Hall
> One to Mrs. Hall, a friend in North Carolina
> Three to Dr. W. P. Beall
> Four to David Harrell
> Parable Letter
> Two to his Daughter Margaret
> To J. O. H. Cosgrave
> One to "Col. Griffith"
> Four to Al. Jennings
> Two to H. P. Steger
> (A few other letters are quoted, in whole or in part, in "Waifs and Strays.")

LICKPENNY LOVER, A. *See:* Voice of the City, The.
"LITTLE SPECK IN GARNERED FRUIT." *See:* Voice of the City, The.
LITTLE TALK ABOUT MOBS, A. *See:* Waifs and Strays.
LITTLE WHITE MAN OF MORLEYS'. *Same as* Assessor of Success.

LOCALITY:

> A geographical arrangement of practically all of the stories. Reference to the book in which the tale appears is given after each title or group of titles.

Central America

> The Head Hunter. (*In* Options)
> Phœbe
> The Fourth in Salvador } *In* Roads of Destiny
> Two Renegades
> The Day We Celebrate. (*In* Sixes and Sevens)

England

Lord Oakhurst's Curse. (*In* Rolling Stones)

France

Roads of Destiny. (*In* Roads of Destiny)
Tracked to Doom. (*In* Rolling Stones)

Mexico

He Also Serves. (*In* Options)

New York

"The Four Million" (Whole volume)
Innocents of Broadway ⎫
A Tempered Wind ⎭ *In* The Gentle Grafter
The Third Ingredient ⎫
Schools and Schools ⎪
Thimble, Thimble ⎪
To Him Who Waits ⎬ *In* Options
No Story ⎪
The Higher Pragmatism ⎪
Rus in Urbe ⎭
The Discounters of Money ⎫
The Halberdier of the Little Rheinschloss ⎬ *In* Roads of Destiny
The Enchanted Profile ⎭
The Marionettes ⎫
A Dinner at—— ⎪
An Unfinished Christmas Story ⎬ *In* Rolling Stones
The Unprofitable Servant ⎭
The Sleuths ⎫
Witches' Loaves ⎪
The Pride of the Cities ⎪
Ulysses and the Dogman ⎪
The Champion of the Weather ⎪
Makes the Whole World Kin ⎪
At Arms with Morpheus ⎪
The Ghost of a Chance ⎬ *In* Sixes and Sevens
Let Me Feel Your Pulse ⎪
The Adventures of Shamrock Jolnes ⎪
The Lady Higher Up ⎪
The Greater Coney ⎪
Transformation of Martin Burney ⎪
The Caliph and the Cad ⎪
The Diamond of Kali ⎭
"Strictly Business." (All the stories in this volume, except A Municipal Report, for which see THE SOUTH under *Tennessee*.)

"The Trimmed Lamp." (Whole volume)
"The Voice of the City." (Whole volume)
Calloway's Code ⎫
"Girl" ⎪
The Marry Month of May ⎪
Sociology in Serge and Straw ⎪
Suite Homes and Their Romance ⎬ *In* Whirligigs
A Sacrifice Hit ⎪
The Song and the Sergeant ⎪
A Newspaper Story ⎪
Tommy's Burglar ⎪
A Little Local Colour ⎭

Pennsylvania (Pittsburgh)

Conscience in Art. (*In* Whirligigs)

South America

"Cabbages and Kings." (Whole volume)
The World and the Door ⎫
The Theory and the Hound ⎬ *In* Options
A Matter of Mean Elevation ⎪
Supply and Demand ⎭
Next to Reading Matter ⎫
A Double-Dyed Deceiver ⎬ *In* Roads of Destiny
On Behalf of the Management ⎭
A Ruler of Men ⎫ *In* Rolling Stones
Helping the Other Fellow ⎭

THE SOUTH—

Alabama

The Ransom of Red Chief. (*In* Whirligigs)

Georgia

Hostages to Momus. (*In* The Gentle Grafter)
"The Rose of Dixie." (*In* Options)

Kentucky

A Blackjack Bargainer. (*In* Whirligigs)
Shearing the Wolf ⎫ *In* The Gentle Grafter
The Ethics of Pig ⎭

Louisiana

The Renaissance at Charleroi ⎫
Whistling Dick's Christmas Stocking ⎬ *In* Roads of Destiny
Cherchez la Femme ⎭
Blind Man's Holiday. (*In* Whirligigs)

Tennessee
A Midsummer Masquerade. (*In* The Gentle Grafter)
October and June. (*In* Sixes and Sevens)
The Whirligig of Life. (*In* Whirligigs)

Virginia
Best Seller. (*In* Options)

Washington
The Hand That Riles the World. (*In* The Gentle Grafter)
A Snapshot at the President. (*In* Rolling Stones)
The Duplicity of Hargraves. (*In* Sixes and Sevens)

Indefinite
The Emancipation of Billy } *In* Roads of Destiny
The Guardian of the Accolade }
The Church With an Overshot Wheel } *In* Sixes and Sevens
The Door of Unrest }

THE WEST—

Arizona
Christmas by Injunction. (*In* Heart of the West)
The Roads We Take. (*In* Whirligigs)

Arkansas
Jeff Peters as a Personal Magnet } *In* The Gentle Grafter
The Man Higher Up }
A Retrieved Reformation. (*In* Roads of Destiny)

Colorado
The Ransom of Mack. (*In* Heart of the West)
The Friendly Call. (*In* Rolling Stones)

Illinois
The Exact Science of Matrimony. (*In* The Gentle Grafter)

Indiana
Modern Rural Sports. (*In* The Gentle Grafter)

Indian Territory
New York by Campfire Light. (*In* Sixes and Sevens)
A Technical Error. (*In* Whirligigs)

Kansas
The Atavism of John Tom Little Bear. (*In* Rolling Stones)

Montana
The Handbook of Hymen. (*In* Heart of the West)

New Mexico
Telemachus, Friend. (*In* Heart of the West)

Oklahoma
Cupid à la Carte. (*In* Heart of the West)
Holding Up a Train. (*In* Sixes and Sevens)

Texas
The Octopus Marooned. (*In* The Gentle Grafter)

Hearts and Crosses
The Pimienta Pancakes
Seats of the Haughty
Hygeia at the Solito
An Afternoon Miracle
The Higher Abdication
The Caballero's Way
The Sphinx Apple } *In* Heart of the West
The Missing Chord
A Call Loan
The Princess and the Puma
The Indian Summer of Dry Valley Johnson
A Chaparral Prince
The Reformation of Calliope

The Hiding of Black Bill
Buried Treasure } *In* Options
The Moment of Victory
A Poor Rule

Art and the Bronco
The Passing of Black Eagle
Friends in San Rosario } *In* Roads of Destiny
The Enchanted Kiss
A Departmental Case
The Lonesome Road

The Marquis and Miss Sally
A Fog in Santone
Tictocq
Aristocracy Versus Hash
A Strange Story } *In* Rolling Stones
Fickle Fortune, or How Gladys Hustled
An Apology
Bexar Script No. 2692

The Last of the Troubadours
Jimmy Hayes and Muriel } *In* Sixes and Sevens
Law and Order
One Dollar's Worth
A Chaparral Christmas Gift
Madame Bo-Peep of the Ranches } *In* Whirligigs
Georgia's Ruling

LONESOME ROAD, THE. *See:* Roads of Destiny.
LORD OAKHURST'S CURSE. *See:* Rolling Stones.
LOST BLEND, THE. *See:* Trimmed Lamp, The.
LOST ON DRESS PARADE. *See:* Four Million, The.
LOTUS AND THE BOTTLE, THE. *See:* Cabbages and Kings.
LOVE-PHILTRE OF IKEY SCHOENSTEIN, THE. *See:* Four Million, The.

M

MADAME BO-PEEP OF THE RANCHES. *See:* Whirligigs.
MADISON SQUARE ARABIAN NIGHT, A. (*A vaudeville sketch has been based on this.*) *See:* Trimmed Lamp, The.
MAKES THE WHOLE WORLD KIN. *See:* Sixes and Sevens.
MAKING OF A NEW YORKER, THE. *See:* Trimmed Lamp, The.
MAMMON AND THE ARCHER. *See:* Four Million, The.
MAN ABOUT TOWN. *See:* Four Million, The.
MAN HIGHER UP, THE. *See:* Gentle Grafter, The.
MARIONETTES, THE. *See:* Rolling Stones.
MARQUIS AND MISS SALLY, THE. *See:* Rolling Stones.
MARRY MONTH OF MAY, THE. *See:* Whirligigs.
MARTIN BURNEY, TRANSFORMATION OF. *See:* Sixes and Sevens.
MASTERS OF ARTS. *See:* Cabbages and Kings.
MATTER OF MEAN ELEVATION, A. *See:* Whirligigs.
MEMENTO, THE. *See:* Voice of the City, The.
MEMOIRS OF A YELLOW DOG. *See:* Four Million, The.
MIDSUMMER KNIGHT'S DREAM, A. *See:* Trimmed Lamp, The.
MIDSUMMER MASQUERADE, A. *See:* Gentle Grafter, The.

MIGNOT, UNPUBLISHED POEMS OF DAVID. *See:* Roads of Destiny, Chap. I.
MIRACLE OF LAVA CAÑON. *Reshaped as* An Afternoon Miracle.
MR. VALENTINE'S NEW PROFESSION. *Same as* Retrieved Reformation, A.
MISSING CHORD, THE. *See:* Heart of the West.
MODERN RURAL SPORTS. *See:* Gentle Grafter, The.
MOMENT OF VICTORY, THE. *See:* Options.
MONEY MAZE. *See:* Cabbages and Kings.
MUNICIPAL REPORT, A. *See:* Strictly Business.
MYSTERY OF THE RUE DE PEYCHAUD, THE, OR TRACKED TO DOOM. *See:* Rolling Stones.

N

NEMESIS AND THE CANDY MAN. *See:* Voice of the City, The.
NEW MANHATTAN NIGHTS. *Name of a series which included* "What You Want?" Discounters of Money, *and* Enchanted Profile.
NEW ORLEANS, STORIES OF. *See:* Under Locality, The South, Louisiana.
NEW YORK BY CAMPFIRE LIGHT. *See:* Sixes and Sevens.
NEW YORK, STORIES OF. *See:* Locality.
NEWSPAPER STORY, A. *See:* Whirligigs.
"NEXT TO READING MATTER." *See:* Roads of Destiny.
NIGHT IN NEW ARABIA, A. *See:* Strictly Business.
NO STORY. *See:* Options.

O

O. HENRY, POEM BY JAMES WHITCOMB RILEY. *See:* Rolling Stones.
OCTOBER AND JUNE. *See:* Sixes and Sevens.
OCTOPUS MAROONED, THE. *See:* Gentle Grafter, The.
ON BEHALF OF THE MANAGEMENT. *See:* Roads of Destiny.

ONE DOLLAR'S WORTH. *See:* Whirligigs.

"ONE ROSE I TWINED WITHIN YOUR HAIR."

> First line of Poem entitled, "The Four Roses" in Roses, Ruses and Romance, a story in "The Voice of the City."

ONE THOUSAND DOLLARS. (*To be the basis of a play.*) *See:* Voice of the City, The.

OPTIONS—SHORT STORIES.

CONTENTS:

"The Rose of Dixie"
The Third Ingredient
The Hiding of Black Bill
Schools and Schools
Thimble, Thimble
Supply and Demand
Buried Treasure
To Him Who Waits

He Also Serves
The Moment of Victory
The Head-Hunter
No Story
The Higher Pragmatism
Best Seller
Rus in Urbe
A Poor Rule

OUT OF NAZARETH. *See:* Waifs and Strays.

P

PASSING OF BLACK EAGLE, THE. *See:* Roads of Destiny.

PAST ONE AT ROONEY'S. (*A vaudeville sketch has been based on this.*) *See:* Strictly Business.

PENDULUM, THE. *See:* Trimmed Lamp, The.

PETERS, JEFF. *See:* Jeff Peters.

PHILISTINE IN BOHEMIA, A. *See:* Voice of the City, The.

PHŒBE. *See:* Roads of Destiny.

PHONOGRAPH AND THE GRAFT, THE. *See:* Cabbages and Kings.

PIMIENTA PANCAKES, THE. *See:* Heart of the West.

PLUNKVILLE PATRIOT, THE.

> Humorous page in *The Rolling Stone*. For photographs of this page see Rolling Stones.

PLUTONIAN FIRE, THE. *See:* Voice of the City, The.

POEMS BY O. HENRY. *See:* Rolling Stones.

O. Henry Index

Titles:

The Pewee
Nothing to Say
The Murderer
Some Postscripts
Two Portraits
A Contribution
The Old Farm

Vanity
The Lullaby Boy
Chanson de Bohème
Hard to Forget
Drop a Tear in this Slot
Tamales

POET AND THE PEASANT, THE. *See:* Strictly Business.

POOR RULE, A. *See:* Options.

PORTER FAMILY, RECORD OF BIRTHS AND DEATHS. *See:* Rolling Stones.

PORTRAITS OF O. HENRY AT VARIOUS AGES. *See:* Rolling Stones.

PRIDE OF THE CITIES, THE. *See:* Sixes and Sevens.

PRINCESS AND THE PUMA, THE. *See:* Heart of the West.

PRISONER OF ZEMBLA, THE. *See:* Rolling Stones.

PROEM, THE: BY THE CARPENTER. *See:* Cabbages and Kings.

PROOF OF THE PUDDING. *See:* Strictly Business.

PSEUDONYMS USED BY O. HENRY: Olivier Henry; S. H. Peters; James L. Bliss; T. B. Dowd; and Howard or Harry Clark.

PSYCHE AND THE PSKYSCRAPER. *See:* Strictly Business.

PURPLE DRESS, THE. *See:* Trimmed Lamp, The.

Q

QUERIES AND ANSWERS. *See:* Rolling Stones.

QUEST OF SOAPY. *Same as* The Cop and the Anthem.

R

RAGGLES. *Same as* Making of a New Yorker, The.

RAMBLE IN APHASIA, A. *See:* Strictly Business.

RANSOM OF MACK, THE. *See:* Heart of the West.

RANSOM OF RED CHIEF, THE. (*To be dramatized.*) *See:* Whirligigs.

RATHSKELLER AND THE ROSE, THE. *See:* Voice of the City, The.

RED ROSES OF TONIA. *See:* Waifs and Strays.
REFORMATION OF CALLIOPE, THE. *See:* Heart of the West.
REMNANTS OF THE CODE, THE. *See:* Cabbages and Kings.
RENAISSANCE AT CHARLEROI, THE. *See:* Roads of Destiny.
REPRODUCTIONS OF MANUSCRIPT AND PAGES FROM THE PLUNKVILLE PATRIOT AS PRINTED BY O. HENRY IN THE ROLLING STONE. *See:* Rolling Stones.
RETRIEVED REFORM. Same as Retrieved Reformation, A.
RETRIEVED REFORMATION, A. (*Dramatized as* "Alias Jimmy Valentine.") *See:* Roads of Destiny.
ROADS OF DESTINY—SHORT STORIES.

CONTENTS:

Roads of Destiny (*To be dramatized*)
The Guardian of the Accolade
The Discounters of Money
The Enchanted Profile
"Next to Reading Matter"
Art and the Bronco
Phœbe
A Double-Dyed Deceiver
The Passing of Black Eagle
A Retrieved Reformation
Cherchez la Femme
Friends in San Rosario
The Fourth in Salvador
The Emancipation of Billy
The Enchanted Kiss
A Departmental Case
The Renaissance at Charleroi
On Behalf of the Management
Whistling Dick's Christmas Stocking
The Halberdier of the Little Rheinschloss
Two Renegades
The Lonesome Road

ROADS WE TAKE, THE. *See:* Whirligigs.
ROBE OF PEACE, THE. *See:* Strictly Business.
ROLLING STONE, THE—O. HENRY'S NEWSPAPER PUBLISHED IN AUSTIN, TEXAS.

Extracts:

Tictocq
Tracked to Doom, or The Mystery of the Rue de Peychaud
A Snapshot at the President
Aristocracy versus Hash
The Prisoner of Zembla
Fickle Fortune or How Gladys Hustled
An Apology

Bexar Scrip No. 2692
Queries and Answers
All of the above will be found in the volume entitled "Rolling Stones."

ROLLING STONES (illustrated).

Stories and Sketches and Poems collected from various magazines, and from *The Rolling Stone*, O. Henry's Texas newspaper.

CONTENTS:

Introduction
The Dream
A Ruler of Men
The Atavism of John Tom Little Bear
Helping the Other Fellow
The Marionettes
The Marquis and Miss Sally
A Fog in Santone
The Friendly Call
A Dinner at——
Sound and Fury—*Dialogue*
Tictocq (from *The Rolling Stone*)
Tracked to Doom, or the Mystery of the Rue de Peychaud (from *The Rolling Stone*)
A Snapshot at the President (Editorial in *The Rolling Stone*)
An Unfinished Christmas Story
The Unprofitable Servant—Unfinished
Aristocracy versus Hash (from *The Rolling Stone*)
The Prisoner of Zembla (from *The Rolling Stone*)
A Strange Story (from *The Rolling Stone*)
Fickle Fortune or How Gladys Hustled (from *The Rolling Stone*)
An Apology (from *The Rolling Stone*)
Lord Oakhurst's Curse (sent in a letter to Dr. Beall, Greensboro, N. C., in 1883)
Bexar Scrip No. 2692 (from *The Rolling Stone*)
Queries and Answers (from *The Rolling Stone*)

Poems:

The Pewee	Vanity
Nothing to Say	The Lullaby Boy
The Murderer	Chanson de Boheme
Some Postscripts	Hard to Forget
A Contribution	Drop a Tear in this Slot
The Old Farm	Tamales

Letters

Some Letters

ROMANCE OF A BUSY BROKER, THE. *See:* Four Million, The.
"ROSE OF DIXIE, THE." *See:* Options.
ROSES, RUSES, AND ROMANCE. *See:* Voice of the City, The.
ROUGE ET NOIR. *See:* Cabbages and Kings.
ROUND THE CIRCLE. *See:* Waifs and Strays.
RUBAIYAT OF A SCOTCH HIGHBALL, THE. *See:* Trimmed Lamp, The.
RUBBER PLANT'S STORY, THE. *See:* Waifs and Strays.
RULER OF MEN, A. *See:* Rolling Stones.
RUS IN URBE. *See:* Options.

S

SACRIFICE HIT, A. *See:* Whirligigs.
SCHOOLS AND SCHOOLS. *See:* Options.
SEATS OF THE HAUGHTY. *See:* Heart of the West.
SERVICE OF LOVE, A. *See:* Four Million, The.
SHAMROCK AND THE PALM, THE. *See:* Cabbages and Kings.
SHAMROCK JOLNES.

A character occurring in The Sleuths and also in The Adventures of Shamrock Jolnes. *See:* Sixes and Sevens

SHEARING THE WOLF. *See:* Gentle Grafter, The.
SHIPS. *See:* Cabbages and Kings.
SHOCKS OF DOOM, THE. *See:* Voice of the City, The.
SHOES. *See:* Cabbages and Kings.
SISTERS OF THE GOLDEN CIRCLE. *See:* Four Million, The.
SIXES AND SEVENS—SHORT STORIES.

CONTENTS:

The Last of the Troubadours
The Sleuths
Witches' Loaves
The Pride of the Cities
Holding Up a Train
Ulysses and the Dogman
The Champion of the Weather
Makes the Whole World Kin
At Arms with Morpheus

The Ghost of a Chance
Jimmie Hayes and Muriel
The Door of Unrest
The Duplicity of Hargraves
Let Me Feel Your Pulse
October and June
The Church with an Overshot Wheel
New York by Campfire Light

The Adventures of Shamrock Jolnes
The Lady Higher Up
The Greater Coney
Law and Order
Transformation of Martin Burney
The Caliph and the Cad
The Diamond of Kali
The Day We Celebrate

SKYLIGHT ROOM, THE. *See:* Four Million, The.
SLEUTHS, THE. *See:* Sixes and Sevens.
SMITH. *See:* Cabbages and Kings.
SNAPSHOT AT THE PRESIDENT, A. *See:* Rolling Stones.
SNOW MAN, THE. *See:* Waifs and Strays.
SOCIAL TRIANGLE, THE. *See:* Trimmed Lamp, The.
SOCIOLOGY IN SERGE AND STRAW. *See:* Whirligigs.
SONG AND THE SERGEANT, THE. *See:* Whirligigs.
SOUND AND FURY—DIALOGUE. *See:* Rolling Stones.
SOUTH AMERICA, STORIES OF. *See:* Locality.
SOUTH, STORIES OF THE. *See:* Locality.
SPARROWS IN MADISON SQUARE, THE. *See:* Waifs and Strays.
SPHINX APPLE, THE. *See:* Heart of the West.
SPRINGTIME À LA CARTE. *See:* Four Million, The.
SQUARING THE CIRCLE. *See:* Voice of the City, The.
STEGER, H. P.

O. Henry's personal friend who edited Rolling Stones and wrote the introduction to the last collection of his works. *See:* Rolling Stones.

STICKNEY'S NECKTIE. *Same as* Unfinished Christmas Story.
STRANGE STORY, A. *See:* Rolling Stones.
STRICTLY BUSINESS—SHORT STORIES.

CONTENTS:

Strictly Business
The Gold That Glittered
Babes in the Jungle

The Day Resurgent
The Fifth Wheel
The Poet and the Peasant

The Robe of Peace
The Girl and the Graft
The Call of the Tame
The Unknown Quantity
The Thing's the Play
A Ramble in Aphasia
A Municipal Report
Psyche and the Pskyscraper
A Bird of Bagdad
Compliments of the Season
A Night in New Arabia
The Girl and the Habit
Proof of the Pudding
Past One at Rooney's
The Venturers
The Duel
"What You Want"

SUCCESSFUL POLITICAL INTRIGUE, A. *See:* Tictocq in Rolling Stones.
SUITE HOMES AND THEIR ROMANCE. *See:* Whirligigs.
SUPPLY AND DEMAND. *See:* Options.

T

TAINTED TENNER, THE TALE OF A. *See:* Trimmed Lamp, The.
TECHNICAL ERROR, A. *See:* Whirligigs.
TELEMACHUS, FRIEND. *See:* Heart of the West.
TEMPERED WIND, A. *See:* Gentle Grafter, The.
TEXAS, STORIES OF. *See:* Locality, Stories of the West.
THANKSGIVING DAY GENTLEMEN, TWO. *See:* Trimmed Lamp, The.
THEORY AND THE HOUND, THE. *See:* Whirligigs.
THIMBLE, THIMBLE. *See:* Options.
THING'S THE PLAY, THE. *See:* Strictly Business.
THIRD INGREDIENT, THE. (*Has been dramatized.*) *See:* Options.
TICTOCQ.

Two French Detective Stories
A Successful Political Intrigue
Tracked to Doom
See: Rolling Stones

TO HIM WHO WAITS. *See:* Options.
TOBIN'S PALM. *See:* Four Million, The.
TOMMY'S BURGLAR. *See:* Whirligigs.

TRACKED TO DOOM, OR THE MYSTERY OF THE RUE DE PEYCHAUD. *See:* Rolling Stones.
TRANSFORMATION OF MARTIN BURNEY, THE. *See:* Sixes and Sevens.
TRANSIENTS IN ARCADIA. *See:* Voice of the City, The.
TRIMMED LAMP, THE—SHORT STORIES.

CONTENTS:

The Trimmed Lamp
A Madison Square Arabian Night
The Rubaiyat of a Scotch Highball
The Pendulum
Two Thanksgiving Day Gentlemen
The Assessor of Success
The Buyer from Cactus City
The Badge of Policeman O'Roon
Brickdust Row
The Making of a New Yorker
Vanity and Some Sables
The Social Triangle
The Purple Dress
The Foreign Policy of Company 99
The Lost Blend
A Harlem Tragedy
"The Guilty Party"—An East Side Tragedy
According to Their Lights
A Midsummer Knight's Dream
The Last Leaf
The Count and the Wedding Guest
The Country of Elusion
The Ferry of Unfulfilment
The Tale of a Tainted Tenner
Elsie in New York

TWO RECALLS. *See:* Cabbages and Kings.
TWO RENEGADES. *See:* Roads of Destiny.
TWO THANKSGIVING DAY GENTLEMEN. *See:* Trimmed Lamp, The.

U

ULYSSES AND THE DOGMAN. *See:* Sixes and Sevens.
UNFINISHED CHRISTMAS STORY, AN. *See:* Rolling Stones.
UNFINISHED STORY, AN. *See:* Four Million, The.
UNKNOWN QUANTITY, THE. *See:* Strictly Business.
UNPROFITABLE SERVANT, THE. *See:* Rolling Stones.

V

VANITY AND SOME SABLES. *See:* Trimmed Lamp, The.
VENTURERS, THE. *See:* Strictly Business.

VITAGRAPHOSCOPE, THE. *See:* Cabbages and Kings.
VOICE OF THE CITY, THE—SHORT STORIES.

CONTENTS:

The Voice of the City
The Complete Life of John Hopkins
A Lickpenny Lover
Dougherty's Eye-Opener
"Little Speck in Garnered Fruit"
The Harbinger
While the Auto Waits
A Comedy in Rubber
One Thousand Dollars
The Defeat of the City
The Shocks of Doom
The Plutonian Fire
Nemesis and the Candy Man
Squaring the Circle
Roses, Ruses, and Romance
The City of Dreadful Night
The Easter of the Soul
The Fool-Killer
Transients in Arcadia
The Rathskeller and the Rose
The Clarion Call
Extradited from Bohemia
A Philistine in Bohemia
From Each According to His Ability
The Memento

W

WAIFS AND STRAYS—SHORT STORIES, AND CRITICAL AND BIOGRAPHICAL MISCELLANY.

CONTENTS:

PART I—*Twelve Stories*

The Red Roses of Tonia
Round the Circle
The Rubber Plant's Story
Out of Nazareth
A Little Talk about Mobs
Confessions of a Humourist
The Sparrows in Madison Square
Hearts and Hands
The Cactus
The Detective Detector
The Dog and the Playlet
The Snow Man

PART II—*Critical and Biographical Comment*

Little Pictures of O. Henry, by Arthur W. Page
The Knight in Disguise, by Nicholas Vachel Lindsay
The Amazing Genius of O. Henry, by Stephen Leacock
O. Henry—an English View, by A. St. John Adcock
The Misadventures in Musical Comedy of O. Henry and Franklin P. Adams
O. Henry in his Own Bagdad, by George Jean Nathan
O. Henry—Apothecary, by Christopher Morley

O. Henry Index

O. Henry, by William Lyon Phelps
About New York with O. Henry, by Arthur B. Maurice
O. Henry and New Orleans, by Caroline F. Richardson
"A Yankee Maupassant"—a Summary of the Early Criticism
O. Henry's Short Stories, by Henry James Forman
The O. Henry Index

WEST, STORIES OF THE. *See:* Locality.
"WHAT YOU WANT." *See:* Strictly Business.
WHERE TO DINE WELL. *See:* A Dinner at—— in Rolling Stones.
WHILE THE AUTO WAITS. *See:* Voice of the City, The.
WHIRLIGIG OF LIFE, THE. *See:* Whirligigs.
WHIRLIGIGS—SHORT STORIES.

CONTENTS:

- The World and the Door
- The Theory and the Hound
- The Hypotheses of Failure
- Calloway's Code
- A Matter of Mean Elevation
- "Girl"
- Sociology in Serge and Straw
- The Ransom of Red Chief
- The Marry Month of May
- A Technical Error
- Suite Homes and their Romance
- The Whirligig of Life
- A Sacrifice Hit
- The Roads We Take
- A Blackjack Bargainer
- The Song and the Sergeant
- One Dollar's Worth
- A Newspaper Story
- Tommy's Burglar
- A Chaparral Christmas Gift
- A Little Local Colour
- Georgia's Ruling
- Blind Man's Holiday
- Madame Bo-Peep of the Ranches

WHISTLING DICK'S CHRISTMAS STOCKING. *See:* Roads of Destiny.
WITCHES' LOAVES. *See:* Sixes and Sevens.
WORLD AND THE DOOR, THE. (*Has been dramatized.*) *See:* Whirligigs.

www.ingramcontent.com/pod-product-compliance
Lightning Source LLC
Chambersburg PA
CBHW011950150426
43195CB00018B/2885